STUDIES IN CONTEMPORARY SOUTHEAST ASIA

CHINA AND SOUTHEAST ASIA SINCE 1945

STUDIES IN CONTEMPORARY SOUTHEAST ASIA

CHINA AND
SOUTHEAST ASIA
SINCE 1945

C. P. FITZGERALD

LONGMAN

Longman Group Limited
London
Associated companies, branches and representatives throughout the world

© Longman Group Limited 1973

ISBN 0 582 12061 6

Typeset by The Universities Press Pty Ltd
Printed in Hong Kong by Dai Nippon Printing Co., (Hong Kong) Ltd

CONTENTS

General Editors' Preface

There is a difficult area between modern history and high journalism which few writers venture into with confidence. Professor C. P. FitzGerald is one of the few because he has done this successfully several times. We were ourselves so confident of the kind of judgment sharpened by experience which he has that we did not give him a terminal date for the period covered in the book. Instead, we encouraged him to come down as far into the present as he could and even to offer some thoughts about the near future. He was first approached to write this book in 1969. He had written most of it by 1971 and reviewed it through 1972 while so much was changing in China's relations with the world and no less in developments in Southeast Asia. The final version went to press well before the Paris agreement was signed permitting the United States to withdraw all its troops from Vietnam. We carefully considered how much this important event would affect Professor FitzGerald's text. But apart from the occasional change of tense where contingency has become fact, there was nothing of substance which was not sound and defensible. We feel that, at this late stage, no change in the text is necessary. Professor FitzGerald, as always, has given us a perceptive interpretation of a long misunderstood subject.

W.G.W.
J.A.C.M.

June, 1973

INTRODUCTION

A consideration of the part played by China in Southeast Asia since 1945 must take into account the fact that China has been concerned with this region for many centuries before the present age. The fact that the former European colonies in the area are now independent states—'new states', as they are somewhat misleadingly often described—obscures the fact that they are for the most part themselves ancient states restored to independence, and still more important, that China is the oldest of them all by many centuries and that her record of contact with these countries runs back far beyond their own recorded history. China is no newcomer to the Southeast Asian scene and her role since 1945 is but the latest chapter in a long continuing story. Not infrequently one can derive the impression from the remarks of Western statesmen that this fact is wholly unknown to them. To put the matter in a comparison which may prove illuminating, if China today were to tell the United Kingdom how far and within what limits Britain should involve herself in the affairs of the neighbouring parts of Europe, blandly assuming that all such interest was recent and a consequence of the late Second World War, we would consider such presumption both ignorant and impertinent. Yet this is the pose which much of Western policy seems to assume in the statements made about China's relations with Southeast Asia.

The relationships between China and the regions to the south date back almost two thousand years. They were confined at first to the countries now comprising Vietnam, North and South, then to Java, Sumatra and the Malay peninsula, and were later extended to Cambodia, Thailand, Burma and the further islands of Indonesia. By the end of the second century A.D., China had established

Fig. 1 Southeast Asia in 1939

frequent diplomatic relations with all the kingdoms then prevailing in these countries and had recorded information about them which is otherwise unavailable. From these contacts there evolved a relationship largely based on trade and the passage of pilgrims from China to India—then the homeland and sacred source of Buddhism—and gradually formalized into a relationship on the official level which followed the pattern then acceptable to rulers and overlords. China invariably treated diplomatic missions from far off countries as tribute bearing missions admitting the suzerainty of the Chinese empire. They were rewarded with even more—often much more— valuable gifts to take home, a form of concealed official trade in valuable commodities. The 'tributary' states were not expected nor required to do more than this, and received no guarantee of aid nor overt alliance in return.

When, centuries later, the Western nations themselves were included in this theoretical system, they tended to resent and reject its implications. It was founded on a concept foreign to their traditions and ideas: that China, the most ancient, the largest, and the most developed political entity of East Asia—the known world of the ancient peoples of this region—was *ipso facto* the leader, the lawgiver, the source of art and culture for all within her orbit. Those who were nearest were therefore expected to conform more closely, as was the case with Korea and Vietnam; those further away, recognized to be more alien, were not required to borrow or adopt so many of China's ways. Tribute and admission of suzerainty were enough. But there could be no equal to the Emperor of China; he was the only truly sovereign ruler in the world. It was a 'constitutional theory', not a working policy. Everyone, from quite early times, knew that in fact there were nations and empires far away which knew not China, and of which China knew but very little. They could be ignored.

The system did not bear harshly upon any state or king. When a king wanted the prestige of China's friendship, to overawe a rival, he sent a tribute mission to the emperor, and received a lavish present in return. When he was not so interested, the system could be ignored for long periods. China was too far away to be a threat and was usually too preoccupied with troubles nearer home to wish to intervene for mere prestige reasons. In later centuries it became a purely formal relationship, and since the end of the Ming naval power and its exercise in the early fifteenth century, it had little real or political significance. Trade continued, was valuable to all parties, but in accordance with Confucian traditional contempt for trade and merchants, was not emphasized nor accorded the importance which in fact it had.

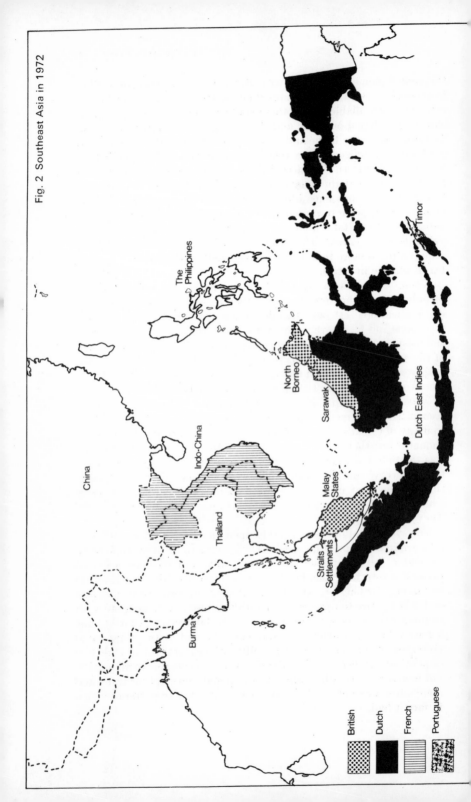

Fig. 2 Southeast Asia in 1972

China

Indo-China

Thailand

Burma

The Philippines

North Borneo

Sarawak

Malay States

Straits Settlements

Dutch East Indies

Timor

British

Dutch

French

Portuguese

The ancient system was destroyed by the active intervention of the Western imperial powers in the nineteenth century. The old relation-ships with Burma, Thailand, the Malay states and the kingdoms of Indo-China, and still more the rather tenuous relationship with the rulers of Indonesia were successively eliminated by the conquests of the European nations. Korea finally fell to the Japanese. All these changes are even today little more than a century old, and in many instances considerably more recent; they can hardly be seen as providing a long established alternative relationship, and the colonial empires themselves have dissolved, giving place to a more familiar and much more ancient pattern of local nation states. China is therefore today confronted with a situation in some ways more normal and governed by an old set of postulates; in another way, novel, and requiring new approaches and making a simple return to old patterns impossible.

The achievement of independence by the former European colonies of Southeast Asia, and the coming to power of the Chinese Communist regime were very nearly contemporary events; they took place within the first decade of the end of the Second World War. Thus a new Southeast Asia was created to confront a new China. In China's relations with the region it is not the few years in which the Nationalist government was declining to its fall—1945 to 1949—that matter; in those years the achievement of independence by Southeast Asian nations was also still incomplete; it is the policies which have emerged since the People's Republic was established on the one side, and the European colonial rulers departed on the other, that have significance.

In this situation there are two main factors: the carry over of old ideas and aspirations from the past, and the adjustment to new situations and developments. For China, the memory of the traditional authority, however lightly exercised it may have been, is connected with the memory of how it was lost—by Western imperial aggression. China has her 'rights'; but these, if implemen-ted, would be in head-on collision with the aspirations of highly nationalist, newly independent peoples, and therefore cannot peaceably be asserted. For the newly independent nations, the old fact is the simple geographic reality that China is there, very large, very powerful, and even more so potentially, and cannot be conjured away. In most of these countries there is another new fact, equally stubborn and potentially controversial, the presence in them of large Chinese minorities, usually economically very strong, which were created in the Colonial period to meet the needs of expanding economies. The capitalist system, in so far as it operates and can continue, depends to a very great degree upon the co-operation and activity of these Chinese communities. The possibility of Communist revolution has also been equated with the strength and potential subversive activity of the Chinese communities. How far this latter belief is substantiated by the facts is a matter to be considered separately in respect of each of these countries. What has hitherto been largely discounted is the question of how far the existence and situation of the various Chinese overseas communities affect the policy of the new China towards them and their host countries, and whether they are not a problem for China as much as for the countries of Southeast Asia.

There is what may perhaps now be called a residual problem: to what extent is the Western world, the former colonial powers including the U.S.A., interested in the future of Southeast Asia and China's relations with that area? An air of unreality now hangs over this question. America fought the Vietnamese Communists claiming that by doing so she was containing 'Chinese Communism'—but China never put an armed man into the struggle. Somewhat nebulous 'presences' are maintained in Southeast Asia by Britain and by Australia, but it is apparent that these are not serious obstacles to Chinese aggression if such should become China's policy. The hope that such small forces will help to maintain stability in the countries of Southeast Asia, and so safeguard the still large investments of the Western former colonial powers, is clearly the main motive; the expectation that they could defend the region against a major onslaught is tacitly abandoned. This gradual development of the remaining Western concern in the area has led the nations of the region to realize that policy towards China must become more realist, less ideologically nationalist, and more circumspect. If China was only a new strong power and not also a Communist one, the making of such policy would be very much easier. But the fact that Mao Tse-tung has proclaimed his régime as the revolutionary model for the underdeveloped world, and that it is, in fact, a model which already shows formidable signs of working towards solutions of the problems of underdevelopment which have so far eluded its Southeast Asian neighbours, gives the question of policy towards China a new and difficult dimension. The relationship between China and these countries is complex, composed of factors coming from the past, of situations created in the interval of colonial domination, and of ideological attitudes and institutions, nationalist and Communist, which often appear irreconcilable.

Chapter One

CHINA AND VIETNAM, CAMBODIA, AND LAOS

1. China and Vietnam

Western people whose interest in Southeast Asia was aroused by events following the end of the Second World War, were, unless they were French, usually unaware of the long connection between China and the present North Vietnam, the former province of Tongking. Yet unless this historical relationship is understood, much of the attitude of the Chinese towards the Vietnamese revolution, and the attitude of the Vietnamese towards China, cannot be explained. China's interest in North Vietnam began in the first century B.C., some two thousand years ago, when the Emperor Wu of the Han dynasty incorporated the territory within his empire following the conquest of the independent state of Nan Yueh, which had its capital at Canton. 'Yueh' is the current northern Chinese pronunciation for the word 'Viet', which has always been the Vietnamese name for themselves.

North Vietnam was then the only part of the modern country thickly settled with people of Viet stock: to the south, in what is now central and southern Vietnam, was the kingdom of Champa, whose inhabitants, the Cham people, were of a very different ethnic origin, probably akin to the peoples of Indonesia. Chinese rule was imposed upon the Viet area, and the area remained under the Han dynasty until the dynasty fell early in third century A.D. The Viet then recovered independence, or rather, autonomy, for their kings acknowledged the suzerainty of the various Chinese dynasties which ruled in the southern half of China between the early fourth century and the beginning of the seventh century—a period when the empire was divided.

The reunited Chinese empire under the T'ang dynasty once more conquered Vietnam and imposed Chinese rule. The country was

renamed *An Nam* (Annam), i.e. the 'Pacified South'. This name
continued in use until the end of French rule, but was never much
liked by the Vietnamese, to whom it typified Chinese conquest. At
the end of the T'ang dynasty, early in the tenth century A.D.,
Vietnam threw off Chinese rule, and became an independent kingdom,
prudently accepting a rather nominal suzerainty of the next great
Chinese dynasty, the Sung. More pacific, or less convinced of the
feasibility of the enterprise, the Sung did not try to conquer Vietnam.
They were contented with suzerainty which left the country to
govern itself. During these centuries of the Sung period, up to the
Mongol conquest in the late thirteenth century, the Vietnamese
people began to expand southwards, at the expense of the kingdom
of Champa, which the Vietnamese ultimately eliminated and
absorbed. Up to this period Vietnam—or Annam—had meant what
is now North Vietnam, the land of the Viet people. 'Vietnam' itself
is a word which reflects the ancient Chinese influence; it means Viet
South, that is the part of the ancient Viet country which was most
southerly from the Chinese point of view. 'South Vietnam' is a
modern term without historical usage.

The Mongols under Khubilai Khan, having conquered the Sung,
went on to try to take Vietnam also. They failed, more on account
of the climate, the jungle and the guerrilla war of the people than
from the defence of the Vietnamese kings, whom they actually
defeated. Vietnam was left to continue in nominal tributary relations with the rulers of China. When the Chinese Ming drove out the
Mongols a hundred years later, they made one attempt to conquer
Vietnam, but finding the resistance obstinate and strong, decided
that the tributary-suzerain relationship was all that was needed,
and withdrew. The last imperial dynasty in China, the Ch'ing
(Manchu) followed this example. China has not ruled in Vietnam
for more than one thousand years. On the other hand the long
connection with China, and the cultural links which this relationship
developed, made Vietnam a region of Chinese civilization, using the
Chinese script, and modelling its institutions on those of the great
empire to the north.

The distinctive feature of Vietnamese culture during this period
of more than one thousand years was its steady expansion southwards. The Chams were despoiled and absorbed, or exterminated.
The most southerly region, the Mekong delta, once part of Cambodia,
was penetrated and finally occupied and incorporated in Vietnam.
Since Vietnamese settlement was thick only on the rice lands, which
in the centre means the narrow coastal plain, the far south, rich and
fertile, and the north, the ancient heart of the kingdom, were
connected by only a narrow waist of settled country. The north was

heavily populated, the far south much less so: migration from the north to the south was the pattern of Vietnamese expansion. For this reason the south retained a kind of colonial atmosphere: life was freer for the peasant immigrant; landlords, although holding large estates, were fewer, and thus less oppressive. Some of the conquered peoples contributed their blood and their character to the southern Vietnamese, not sufficiently to mark them off as a different people, but enough to give them a distinct regional nature. In the fifteenth and sixteenth centuries this was reflected in the establishment of a southern viceroyalty which, as the royal power in Hanoi declined, assumed something of an independent political status. The centre of this viceroyalty was the city of Hué, in central Vietnam.

At the end of the eighteenth century, following civil wars and rebellions, it was the heir of the southern viceroys who, with some French help, reunited the whole country, north and south alike, and moved the capital to Hué, the traditional seat of his own family's power. Whatever may be thought of the manner of his government, which was arbitrary, it is certain that the reunion of the whole country was popular, and had been the objective of the great popular rebellion which had in effect destroyed the old royal dynasty in Hanoi. When during the nineteenth century French penetration gradually undermined this unity, first by the annexation of the far south which was named by the French Cochin-China (a name unknown to the Vietnamese language), the unrest and resentment of the people were largely directed against this dismemberment of the nation. The 'empire' of Annam, as it was now called, was finally confined to the central provinces, and even the north, the ancient kingdom, although still nominally a province of the empire, was placed under direct French rule. The empire itself was now a French protectorate, all real power resting with the colonial authorities.

China had not concerned itself with the rise and fall of Vietnamese dynasties. But when the French forced the Vietnamese monarch to renounce the suzerainty of China, revolt broke out in the north (1883), and received Chinese support. The Franco-Chinese War of 1883-5 ended in a French victory, not without encountering some sharp setbacks in north Vietnam, and China had to renounce her suzerainty over Vietnam, which had then lasted for nearly one thousand years. French authority was extended to a protectorate over neighbouring Cambodia and then to Laos, the whole French dominion being now known as Indo-China. It was never unopposed in Vietnam; conspiracies, rebellions, and unrest continued throughout the period of French rule. So, too, did the movement of the Vietnamese people to the south. The development of rubber estates and the large scale cultivation of rice for the world market, created a demand for labour in the south, which was met by Vietnamese immigration extending into Cambodia. At the same time, the introduction of a form of the Latin alphabet to write the Vietnamese language diminished the cultural link with China, although the older generation clung to the Chinese script and literature as a mark of status. French became the second language of the educated class (but not of the peasantry) and a new generation of French trained civil servants, confined to lower ranks, replaced the old 'mandarins' of Chinese education. The new élite, however, was also strongly nationalist, and its opposition to French rule took on more modern forms than the conservative, monarchical standpoint of the 'mandarins'.

When Japan first occupied Vietnam in 1941, following the defeat of France in Europe, the French administration was left to govern in civil affairs, while military power passed to the Japanese. By the time that Japan surrendered in August 1945 the French authorities had lost both prestige and control; nationalist Vietnamese, of varying political allegiances, took up arms and seized power, both in north and south. The Emperor Bao Dai attempted to lead the nation to total independence, but was unable to rally a majority to his cause. In the south the Vietminh movement, Communist led, seized Saigon, but were ejected by allied forces (mainly British) sent in to take the Japanese surrender. Saigon was handed over to the returning French, but resistance continued in the countryside. Under the terms of the Japanese surrender, the north of Vietnam, the province of Tongking down to the 16th parallel of latitude, was allotted to the Commander-in-Chief of the China War Zone for occupation and for the repatriation and disarmament of the Japanese forces in that region. The Commander-in-Chief of the China War Zone was General Chiang Kai-shek, head of the Chinese Republic, and it was his troops who entered North Vietnam, occupying Hanoi and all other chief cities to disarm the Japanese. After sixty years of French rule, the Chinese were back in north Vietnam again, but they did not intend to stay forever.

The Vietminh movement, under Ho Chi Minh, had been active in resistance to the Japanese invasion; it therefore claimed the status of an allied resistance movement, and had in fact received arms and some munitions from the allied forces in East Asia. The Chinese authorities co-operated with Ho Chi Minh, since their own policy was to frustrate any re-establishment of French power in North Vietnam, at least that part of the country which has common frontiers with China. It was under the Chinese occupation, and with the full consent of the occupying power, that Ho Chi Minh set up in Hanoi the government of the Republic of Vietnam, to which many people of differing political views rallied as the centre of national resurgence most likely to achieve the independence of the whole country. Bao Dai abdicated and took office under the new government. It should be emphasised that the Chinese government which furthered and countenanced this move in the territory it occupied was that of Chiang Kai-shek, who was himself in the next year to enter into a desperate and disastrous civil war against the Chinese Communist Party. Although the Hanoi government was not officially known as a Communist Republic, everyone knew that Ho Chi Minh was a Communist and that the Vietminh movement was Communist controlled.

The French negotiated for their return to North Vietnam; changing governments in Paris led to changes of policy, and finally to a breakdown in the negotiations. The French attacked Hanoi and Haiphong, occupied those cities, and were thus launched into the first phase of the Vietnamese war, both in north and south, which was to continue with increasing lack of success until ended by the Geneva Conference of 1954. Meanwhile, China had withdrawn her troops, which were indeed needed to meet the Communist challenge. It was not until late in 1949, after the final victory of the Communist armies on the mainland that these armies, and the authority of the newly proclaimed People's Republic of China, reached the border with Vietnam. By that time it was four years since Ho Chi Minh had set up his government in Hanoi, and three years since, driven from the cities, he had begun conducting war against the French throughout the countryside. The rise of the Communist regime in North Vietnam thus took place under the Nationalist Chinese occupation, and in the years following the end of the occupation, but before the Chinese Communists had taken over the south China provinces bordering on Vietnam. The aims of Chiang's policy were never made clear or public. Probably the objectives were to keep the French from regaining power and to permit, if not to sustain, a Vietnamese regime which helped this purpose, even if it was of left wing character. Chiang hoped to win the civil war and crush his own Communists; thereafter he might have been ready to help a non-Communist nationalist movement in Vietnam to power. He never had the opportunity to pursue any such policy.

The Chinese Communist regime naturally had a close sympathy with the Vietminh movement, which was Communist led and increasingly Communist in policy. Ho Chi Minh was personally well known to the Chinese Communist leaders and was an old revolutionary comrade. There can be little doubt that the Chinese hoped for a victory by the Vietminh, and were ready to enter into friendly relations with a Communist Vietnamese government. At this period the war, spreading to all parts of Vietnam, north and south, was seen as a national resistance against French rule, led by Communists, but supported by the great majority of the nation. No idea of dividing the country into North and South had arisen. China had just emerged from a long civil war, which in turn had followed close upon the Japanese invasion. The following year, 1950, was to see the outbreak of the Korean War, and China's involvement in that conflict against forces primarily American. It was clearly not a time when China could contemplate an active policy of intervention in Vietnam, even if this had been essential to save the Vietminh movement from defeat. But there was no such danger; the French, in spite of massive American assistance with arms, were losing the war. French opinion at home was weary of the useless struggle, and divided as to its aims and justification. The Chinese frontier provided a sure line of supply for the Vietminh, and contact with the outer world. This was all that was required of China at that time. The Vietminh would, and did, do the rest. China could also give diplomatic support and recognition to the government of Ho Chi Minh, and the latter step was taken in January 1950. In consequence, France refused to recognize the People's Republic of China, and did not do so until 1964, long after the First Vietnam War.

The years from 1950, when the Korean War began, until 1953, when the protracted armistice negotiations at Panmunjom finally brought the conflict to a lasting ceasefire, although not to any settlement embodied in a treaty, saw a constant deterioration in the French military situation in Vietnam. During these same years China was involved firstly in the heavy fighting of the war in North Korea, and then as a party to the armistice negotiations which did not at times seem likely to arrive even at a ceasefire. At this period, only three to four years after the Chinese Communists had taken power, China was still in the early stages of the reconstruction of the ruined economy and devastation caused by the Japanese invasion, the civil war, and the inept policies of the former Nationalist government. China was very largely dependent on Russia for armaments and all forms of technical assistance, and industrial technology. Policy had therefore to be made to fit these facts: it was not yet possible for China to follow a foreign policy differing in important respects from that of the Soviet Union. Russia was more concerned with the Korean War and its outcome than with the distant struggle in Vietnam; moreover, placing hopes in the development of the internal politics of the Fourth Republic in France itself, which were complex and unstable, Russia was not anxious to place the French Communist Party in a disadvantageous electoral position, as might be the consequence of open support for the Vietminh in their war against the French colonial regime. For these reasons it was equally necessary for China also to pursue a moderate policy in respect of the Vietnamese war.

A further reason for keeping aid to Vietnam indirect and avoiding a military commitment was the need to avoid arousing the recent memories of the Nationalist Chinese occupation in 1945. The Vietnamese have always shown suspicion and some hostility to all Chinese armed forces, of any political colour. Those of Chiang Kai-shek, which at the time of their occupation numbered no less than 120,000, had left behind a bad reputation for commandeering rice stores without payment, corruption and outright looting. While the forces of the People's Republic were far better disciplined, it still remained true that they would be Chinese, speaking a different language, and aliens in the eyes of the Vietnamese. The very essence of the Vietminh movement was to recover the independence of the country, to get rid of all foreign domination; the too open aid of yet another foreign army would have been politically of slight advantage, and might have proved harmful.

Indirect aid, the supply of weapons and ammunition, the training of men to use sophisticated weapons, and the use of neighbouring Chinese territory to provide rest and recreation areas and to supply food, was the method which both sides agreed would be most suitable. China recognized the Democratic Republic of Vietnam, and was thus within her legal rights to supply that government with what it wished to obtain. To assert that this doctrine applies only to the other side—that is the U.S.A. recognized the French government, it was thus within its rights to give massive aid in munitions to France, but that China had no similar right to help Vietnam—is to support the type of misleading claim that has continued to confuse the real issues of the war in Vietnam.

There is no doubt that in respect of China the Republic of Vietnam, that is the Vietminh movement, enjoyed one major advantage. The territory of the two countries adjoins; there are passes through the mountains, and there are roads, even if at this time they were bad roads, connecting the two countries. It was, and no doubt still is, very easy for China to supply Vietnam by these routes, which cannot be closed except by violation of Chinese territory. Any such violation would involve bringing China into the war, a consequence from which the French government shrank, and one which the U.S.A., in the second phase of the Vietnam War, has also avoided.

Late in 1953 the development of the last major French offensive to crush the Vietminh in northern Vietnam led to the establishment of a strong French force in the isolated valley of Dienbienphu. There it was before long besieged, and cut off from land communications with Hanoi, then in French hands. Early in 1954 the various powers most concerned with the prolonged war in Vietnam decided to call a conference to try to achieve a peaceful settlement. The motives of the different countries who attended the Geneva Conference have been much discussed. The British government, concerned at the wastage of French power, and its possible consequences in Europe, was anxious to achieve any settlement which would enable the French to withdraw from what was clearly a losing struggle with dignity and the least possible sacrifice of prestige and power. The Russians, on the other side, had their own reservations about pushing France too hard. They wished to conserve their influence with the powerful French Communist Party, and if France was humiliated, this situation might react unfavourably upon the electoral prospects of that Party. China, at this time hardly a wholly free agent, and in the need to conform with Russian views, supported this more moderate line. On the other hand the U.S.A., where the State Department was conducted by Mr John Foster Dulles, was committed to an unyielding anti-Communist stance. Dulles wanted the Conference merely to register the failure of peace negotiations as a prelude to massive intervention by the Western powers, mainly with air power, to save the French and win the war. Most of the smaller participant powers took the line of the British government, while in France itself, a right wing government, committed to the American policy, was rapidly losing popularity and support. Mr Dulles, refusing even to meet the Chinese delegate, the Foreign Minister, Chou En-lai, face to face, left the Conference when he realized that his views would not prevail. It seemed that the Conference must fail. At this point, in early May 1954, the defenders of Dienbienphu, at the end of their supplies, were forced to capitulate. A major factor in this Vietnamese victory was the use of Chinese supplied artillery, which prevented the French air lifting of supplies into the besieged camp.

The French government resigned; its successor, under M Mendes-France was from the first determined to end the war, and as this meant in practice withdrawing from Vietnam, indeed from all Indo-China, the decision was courageous. It was strongly supported by French public opinion. The Conference thus was able to continue, and to conclude in July 1954 two accords, which left much unclarified and gave rise to many difficulties later. A ceasefire was signed between the French (not any Vietnamese authority of the south) and the Democratic Republic of Vietnam, which in contemporary speech is usually known as North Vietnam. By the terms of this agreement the armies were to regroup, the Vietnamese armies north of the 17th parallel of latitude, the French to withdraw, and the South Vietnamese forces hitherto in French service were to be placed under the command of a newly organized government in Saigon which would take over from the French. By July 1956 at the latest, as it was expressly laid down, elections would be held to determine the political future of the whole country. There was no suggestion of a permanent partition between North and South.

It is known that this agreement owed much to the persuasion of the Chinese delegation, as was acknowledged by Mr Eden, then Foreign Secretary, in the House of Commons. The Vietminh leaders were rather unwilling to evacuate large areas in the south where they had fought for years, and where their military position justified the hope of victory. But both Russia and China succeeded in convincing Ho Chi Minh that half a loaf was better than no bread, and that in any case, as they had the backing of the mass of the people, elections would ensure their future political victory. This was also the opinion of U.S. President Eisenhower, who committed himself to the statement that 80 per cent of the voters would support the Vietminh. Elections would thus secure the victory of the Vietminh without further devastating war, and also, it was assumed, avoid the risk of further foreign intervention.

It is well known that these hopes were frustrated.

The first phase, following the French withdrawal seemed to hold out some prospect of lasting peace. The successor government in Saigon was incompetent, rent by factions, and unable to keep peace. It would, without foreign aid, have soon collapsed. But the U.S.A. had refused to sign the accords at Geneva, although 'taking note' of them. American policy was not bound by them, and soon worked openly against them. Ngo Din Diem, a right wing nationalist politician long an exile in the U.S.A., was brought back to head the Saigon government, and given ample backing. Before long he compelled the Emperor Bao Dai to abdicate and proclaimed a Republic—which claimed to be the legal government of the whole country, not merely of South Vietnam. Thus the terms South and North Vietnam have no validity in any part of the country. Neither side accepts the partition as legal, and the leaders of the South, especially Air Marshal Ky, have more than once made this standpoint plain in public utterances. No elections were held. Diem claimed that they would not be free in the North, but did not on that account hold any himself in the South. This attitude, which nullified one of the most important parts of the Geneva agreements, received, and has continued to receive, endorsement from the U.S.A. In North Vietnam and in China it was regarded as a breach of a solemn undertaking, and as rendering the whole agreement null and void. This is the genesis of the Second Vietnam War.

In 1960 following the constant and brutal repression of the Diem regime uprisings began in the new South Vietnam state. The insurgents formed the National Liberation Front, which contained many who were not Communists, but which has at all times been led by the Communist Party. It gained widespread support, and by 1963 was within sight of victory. Meanwhile U.S. involvement grew in strength and depth; when the Diem government was overthrown by strong internal opposition, leading to the slaying of the dictator and his brother, the U.S. supported a series of further military dictators and increased the American forces committed to the war. From 1960 onward there has been a continuing war, fought more and more on the one side by massive American forces, and on the other by the so called 'Viet Cong', a term which is an abbreviation for the Vietnamese words for Vietnam Communist Party, but is not the official name for the National Liberation Front which carries on the war in South Vietnam. North Vietnam regular army forces have been engaged, often in strength, and from 1964 to 1968 the U.S. carried on a sustained and very heavy aerial attack on North Vietnam, until this was terminated by President Johnson shortly before he resigned his candidacy for the next Presidency (1 April 1968).

The second phase of the Vietnam War has not directly involved China. American intervention has been justified in propaganda by the claim that by fighting 'Communism' in Vietnam, Chinese ambitions and activity in the region are contained. In other words that China would be in control of this part of Southeast Asia if the Vietnamese Communists came to power. There is no evidence yet produced for any such conclusion; it is very well known to all students of East Asia and its history that Chinese intervention in Vietnam has been resisted and finally rejected for the past thousand years. China has at no time sent troops into Vietnam, nor aircraft; nor have her forces been involved in any more than a small number of isolated clashes with any American forces operating in Vietnam. These incidents arose from American aircraft which, losing their bearings, flew over Chinese territory. Neither side has made them into an issue of substance. If the relations between China and Vietnam in this second phase are to be considered objectively, this myth must be laid aside.

From the point of view of China the second phase of the war has certainly posed some difficult problems. Firstly, the Vietnamese have not really concealed their view that they were pressured into an agreement at Geneva in 1954, which was less favourable than they had the right to expect, and was moreover then dishonoured in its most significant aspect, the elections scheduled 'by 1956 at the latest'. China has had to make amends for what must now be admitted to have been an error of judgement, or alternatively, a somewhat opportunist and selfish attitude. The fact that China was then conforming to Russian policy may, in the years which have seen the

Sino-Russian dispute develop, provide an excuse to saddle the blame upon the U.S.S.R. but this alters nothing. China is thus morally bound to render Vietnam all the aid that can be provided, or needed, to maintain the struggle. China has in fact fulfilled this task, and a large part of the arms used by the Vietnamese Communist forces, north and south, come from China. As their opponents are wholly supplied by America it can hardly be said to be a one-sided participation. China has also supplied food, especially during the period when intense American bombardment of the North Vietnamese countryside was interrupting or delaying the movement of supplies. China has, in fact taken the position that she will give Vietnam all aid short of military involvement, which there seems no reason to believe was ever desired by the Vietnamese Communists.

The Chinese have certainly other reasons than their obligations to Vietnam for taking this course, and sustaining the war against America. For several years, until the recent changes in American opinion and the growing disapproval of the war became open and expressed, American policy appeared to envisage that in certain circumstances the war could spread to China herself. These views were expressed by American 'hawks' and if never endorsed by official statements, were equally not denied by any positive directive on policy. It is certain that the risk was taken seriously by the Chinese after President Johnson's escalation of the war in 1965. It would, indeed, have been a rather over confident government, not to say a careless one, which would have ignored this risk. The sustained bombardment of North Vietnam could be interpreted as a preliminary to the invasion of that part of the country by land forces also. This would have brought American forces to the frontier of China; no one can be sure that in this situation further involvement would not have brought China into direct conflict with the U.S.A. There is reason to think that this possibility was expected and indeed regarded as inevitable by some sections of the Chinese leadership. One of the last public pronouncements by the subsequently deposed and criticised Head of State Liu Shao-ch'i, in June 1966, was to declare to the Vietnamese that they could count upon China as their 'rear area'. Lo Jui-ch'ing, then chief of the Chinese staff, but subsequently dismissed and criticized in the Cultural Revolution, is believed to have supported the more bellicose party which was ready to fight the U.S. and probably believed that such a conflict could not be avoided.

Thus, the more the Americans were bogged down in Vietnam, the less they achieved by the bombardment of North Vietnam, and the more the Chinese could feel delivered of danger. But there was the risk that this frustration might work the other way; that unable to overcome either the North Vietnamese regime by bombardment, nor

the guerrillas by 'search and destroy' operations, the President would
be advised that the only solution was the invasion of North Vietnam
and south China, so as to deny the Vietnamese the close support of
Chinese territory. China could not withdraw her support from
Vietnam without a very serious loss of authority, confidence and
national status. It would seem that the contest between those who
believed that the American war was inevitable, and should be fought
in the first place on conventional lines—such as General Lo Jui-
ch'ing—and those who in any case thought that China should pursue
a strategy of massive extended guerrilla war, luring the enemy deep
into the country, but avoiding set battles, was an underlying factor
in the bitterness of the Cultural Revolution.

There was more to this dispute than the simple question of which
military plan would be best in an inevitable war; there is reason to
think that Mao Tse-tung and some of those closely associated with
him, such as the Defence Minister Lin Piao, did not accept the
inevitability of the war with the U.S.A. whatever they might be
saying in public. It was their plan to adopt widespread guerrilla
tactics—protracted war, as Mao phrases it—not only because these
would be the most effective against U.S. air power and artillery
superiority, but even more because the very prospect of such a war
was very likely to discourage all but the most dedicated 'hawks'
from running any risk of it. America was already, in 1966, clearly
failing to win the war, or to accomplish even after two years by the
bombardment of North Vietnam what the experts to whom President
Johnson had listened had promised him—North Vietnam's capitulation or suing for peace within two months. It was thus probable
that the prospect of repeating this frustrating experience on a scale
twenty times as great at least—the bombardment and invasion of
China—would not appeal to any U.S. leader as a possible solution.
The war in Vietnam and the resistance to aerial bombardment of the
North Vietnamese population was therefore a prime interest for
China—to discourage the Americans from doing the same thing in
China.

It is of course well known that this interpretation is not readily
acceptable in the West. The understanding of what Chinese fears, as
opposed to Chinese menaces, may be, has never been conspicuous or
brought before public attention by statesmen and publicists. But it
is necessary to take account of the facts if Chinese policy towards
Vietnam is to be understood. It must also be recognized that Mao
Tse-tung's assessment of the situation was more correct than that of
his opponents. There has been no Sino-American war; indeed, in
the years of the Cultural Revolution in so far as Sino-American
relations moved at all, it was to a somewhat more relaxed mood.

On the other hand, China was manifestly not seeking any confrontation, even when engaging in polemical and ideological extravagances. Incidents between U.S. aircraft and Chinese ground gunners decreased, rather than increased in these years. Secondly, the acerbity of the Sino-Soviet dispute seemed to preoccupy the Chinese to the exclusion of other aspects of foreign policy, and in some measure thus decreased tension with the U.S.A. China, indeed, had no reason as far as Vietnam was concerned to change her policy. Vietnamese resistance continued, and if anything grew more effective. There was no need to inject any new and potentially dangerous factor into this situation.

On the part of the U.S. it may well be that the Chinese policy of preparing for protracted war if invaded, and letting it be known very clearly that that was their policy, was understood and appreciated. The time when such a campaign might have been contemplated had probably passed away with the Dulles era. Since that time America may have become deeply involved in East Asia, but more by mistakes than by deliberate decisions. In April 1968, eighteen months after the Cultural Revolution began in China, President Johnson called the halt to the bombing of North Vietnam, renounced his candidacy for the Presidency in the election of that year, and set in motion the process of American withdrawal from Vietnam which his successor has also adopted and more or less implemented. The basic cause of this decision may have been the disillusionment of the American people, especially manifest since the Tet offensive by the Vietnamese Communists in February 1968 demonstrated the falsity of the picture which propaganda was presenting of the course of the war, or it may have been the fact that a sounder military judgement had assessed the real magnitude of the policy of conquest, and had advised that it was too high a price to pay. But whatever the cause, the decision to withdraw has fundamentally altered the situation in which Chinese relations with Vietnam are conducted.

It may be too soon to say that the Vietnamese War is coming to an end; its recent extension into Cambodia makes any such assumption very uncertain; but it is clear that the policy of 'Vietnamization' designed to make it possible for the American forces to leave the country without actually surrendering it to the Vietnamese Communists creates a new situation. It will soon no longer be possible to maintain the argument that this is not a civil war but an aggression by one sovereign state upon another, an argument which has never been really accepted by any Vietnamese party or group. It will become very plainly a civil war, without the participation of foreign troops. What the outcome of that change may be cannot be known, but it is generally considered that in the past the South Vietnamese army could not, or would not, effectively resist the Communist forces, and the justification for the intervention of half a million American troops was that without this vast deployment of aid, Saigon would have lost the war. It must be assumed that the Chinese, the North Vietnamese, and the Vietnamese Communists in the south (as well as many other observers) believe that the character of the Saigon forces has not so greatly changed as to make this previous estimation of their strength invalid now.

China, for the time being, appears to be continuing her former policy; she is supplying the Vietnamese with weaponry and with needed supplies. The spread of the war to Cambodia will probably make this necessary for some time, perhaps for some years, but if the American withdrawal continues, and the Saigon army fights on in Cambodia and in its own country, it seems very possible that the victory of the Communist side, so often postponed but never prevented, will be achieved. China will then need to frame a policy in which a new, probably unified, Communist Vietnam is the other partner. On the experience of the past this will need to be a relationship much more nearly of equals than of patron and client. So far from China dominating a Communist Vietnam, it is more probable that Communist Vietnam will pursue its own ambitions in Southeast Asia, which may not necessarily wholly coincide with those of China.

An aspect of Chinese relations with the Democratic Republic of Vietnam (North Vietnam) which cannot be overlooked is that these relations, and Chinese aid to the Communist side in the Vietnam War, have become involved in the Sino-Soviet dispute. Russian aid comes to Vietnam both by sea, to the port of Haiphong, and by land across China, by rail down to Hanoi. During the Cultural Revolution, and even shortly before, there were incidents when China was accused by the Russians of delaying the transport of supplies and munitions destined for Hanoi in transit across China. The background of this aspect of the quarrel has never been made clear, but it was apparently solved, or eased, by a new arrangement by which North Vietnamese officials stationed at the Chinese frontier with Russia, in North Manchuria, took delivery of the consignments there, and they were then transported across China as Vietnamese goods, not as Russian aid material. This may seem a rather transparent device, but probably reflected a need to avoid public exhibition of Russian insignia and ownership at a time when public opinion had been inflamed against the Soviet Union. At this time, and subsequently, the Chinese propaganda has continued to allege that Russia was in collusion with the U.S.A., and half-hearted in her support of the Communist forces in Vietnam. The open evidence of Russian aid to Hanoi could have spread doubt about the veracity of this charge.

In reality, as is well known, Russia has supplied to the Communist forces most of the more sophisticated weapons which they use. Rockets, interceptor missiles, and much else is of Russian make and origin. The Chinese have supplied small arms, mortars and less complicated weapons. The reason is obvious: China can make these types in profusion, but her output of the advanced type of weapon is much more limited, and probably required for her own forces. Russia, at a great distance from Vietnam, finds it more useful to supply smaller quantities of advanced types of weapons. There is no cause for dispute about this situation, other than the existing quarrel between China and Russia, which leads both sides to try to score points off the other by claiming that their aid is insufficient, or insincere. Hanoi, in need of both, has managed with great skill to avoid taking sides.

Equally, neither the Chinese nor the Russians can afford to leave North Vietnam and the National Liberation Front in the lurch. China has a direct national interest in preserving an independent and Communist Vietnam, if possible throughout the country, so as to deny to America any area which could be used as a land base in war with China. This consideration is paramount to Chinese policy, and probably much more important than any possibility of exercising strong influence in Hanoi after the war is over. If the Chinese really hoped to dominate a Communist Vietnam and exclude Russian influence, the course of the war should have disillusioned them. At no time has Hanoi been willing to criticize either side, and at all times Hanoi has welcomed Russian aid as well as Chinese. If this independent line was possible when the country was under daily aerial bombardment by U.S. forces and engaged in a deadly struggle in the countryside of Vietnam, it is clear that once the whole country is united under the Vietnamese Communists' rule, they would be in a much stronger position still to maintain an independent policy.

The Vietnamese Communists, north or south, have not attempted to emulate the Chinese Cultural Revolution. There has been no such movement in Vietnam. Even if they were attracted to these ideals (of which they have made no public sign), the time would be very unsuitable for any such upheaval. But Mao Tse-tung, in his propaganda for home consumption, has continued to stress that only by following the path he has laid down can Communist regimes avoid the pitfall of 'revisionism' into which he thinks the Russian leadership has fallen. This suggests that China is mainly concerned to preserve the Communist state in Vietnam, and not to control it. Whether, the Vietnamese Communists, once victorious, would wish to start their own Cultural Revolution is far from certain, and on the whole not very likely. They would be occupied for many years in restoring a devastated country, a task for which they will need all the foreign aid they can get. This must come mainly from Russia and from China. It will be just as essential to avoid quarrelling with either of the two great friends in peace as it has been in war.

Russian aims in Vietnam are also, it would seem, limited. The country is very distant from the Soviet Union, and it has always shown a strong national identity which is hostile to foreign control or even to overriding foreign influence. But it is a Communist state, and victory for the Democratic Republic and the National Liberation Front would lead before long to the unification of the country under Communist rule. Russia cannot afford to allow America to destroy a Communist state, or to crush a strong Communist movement such as the National Liberation Front. On the other hand as long as the Americans continue to fight a war which cannot be won, they are deeply committed to Vietnam, and proportionately distracted from regions such as the Middle East which are of more direct concern to Russian interests. It may well be that the Russians are not very distressed at the continuance of the war. Their aid can keep the Vietnamese fighting indefinitely; there is good reason to believe that the American people are not prepared to undertake a similar open ended commitment in Vietnam.

These considerations are clearly now well understood in Washington. The policy of withdrawal amounts to a recognition that the war cannot be won, and is based on the hope that the armies of Saigon can carry it on sufficiently effectively to make a negotiated settlement seem better than endless war to the Vietnamese Communists. On the other hand, evidence that this hope could be realized is not convincing. It is suggested that President Nixon seeks to escape from Vietnam by 'Vietnamization' not in the belief that this affords an alternative way to victory, or even to a compromise solution, but because an end to the war, in effect by Communist victory, would be acceptable to the new mood in the U.S.A. so long as it did not involve the open capitulation of American forces in the field. If Saigon succumbs after the Americans have left the country, the blame can be laid upon the deficiencies of that regime which, if it had true popular support, would be able to survive.

This prospect is still somewhat remote; the Americans have not all gone, and the incursion into Cambodia left new problems. It is true that the Americans limited their commitment to the Cambodian expedition, and withdrew from that country after a brief period. But they did permit the entry of the Saigon forces, which did not withdraw when the Americans went. The war thus spread to a new country and new fronts; in that situation it is uncertain, at least, whether Saigon possesses the resources to carry it on, or the capacity to achieve success. The Cambodian venture has proved divisive in America and has been almost universally deplored in other parts of the world. The presence of the Saigon army in Cambodia, among its traditional enemies the Khmer people (Cambodians), is distrusted and disapproved by other Asian countries, and gives the Communist side very valuable moral support. It also enhances the influence of China in the region.

China has recognized the government in exile of Prince Norodom Sihanouk, the former Chief of State of Cambodia. Whatever transgressions he may have committed, he remains a figure respected and often admired throughout the Asian world, and it is already all too clear that his removal from power has been a calamity to his country and people. It is not at all unlikely that he will regain control, at least in a large part of the country, and he will owe this restoration to the active assistance of the Communist Vietnamese and to China in the background. It would seem very probable that in that event he would rely upon China for aid and support more than on the Vietnamese Communists, given the long standing antipathy between Khmers and Vietnamese of all colours. This is no doubt one reason why the U.S.S.R. has not followed China in recognizing Prince Sihanouk's government in exile, which moreover, has its seat at Peking.

The essential fact about relations now or in the future, as in the past, between China and Vietnam is the proximity of the two countries. Whatever happens they must still be neighbours; whether on good terms or bad, at war or at peace, Vietnam and China are linked by geography. No such imperative dictates the relations of either Russia or the U.S.A. with this country. Both are far away, neither has any national interest at stake. Their concern is purely ideological; whether Vietnam is 'lost' to Communism, as the Americans used to say, or defended from 'imperialism' as the Russians would maintain. A settlement which permitted both Russia and the U.S. to disengage from the Vietnamese question would be a relief to both powers. But neither can yet agree to a settlement which is clearly unfavourable to it, and a success for the opponent.

The Chinese position is fundamentally different from this; for China, Vietnam is a neighbour, occupying a strategic situation which in the hands of an inimical regime could be a danger, and in the hands of friends, or even of a strongly neutral government, is a front line of defence, which could be left to order its own affairs so long as no alien foreign influence is admitted. The whole history of Vietnam shows that the Vietnamese themselves would oppose any such foreign influence that threatened to dominate their country. Therefore for China, whether the future regime in Vietnam follows the

'Thought of Mao Tse-tung', or prefers to adopt a less ideological form of Communism is not really important. Independent Communist Vietnam can be relied upon to oppose any strong foreign domination by an alien power, whether Communist or not.

Vietnam is a closely settled country in the fertile regions; for centuries the Vietnamese themselves have been an expanding people, occupying and colonizing the formerly empty southern part of the country. There is no room here for massive Chinese colonization or the formation of a large minority Chinese community, such as has grown up in Malaysia and in Thailand. Chinese control would raise enmity and resistance, as it did in the past. Also, since the reforms which made the Vietnamese language dominant in literature as well as in common speech, and now written in the Latin alphabet and no longer in Chinese ideographs, Chinese cultural influence cannot be as strong as it was in the old kingdom of Vietnam where literature was in effect a local Chinese literature and education was modelled on Chinese culture and Confucian ethics. If both countries will be under Communist rule, that will be a bond, but not necessarily a Chinese domination even in the intellectual and cultural sense.

Should the Vietnam War end in some compromise which still allows a non-Communist government to survive in some part of South Vietnam, it is unlikely that this solution would prove lasting. Such a regime, whether headed by President Thieu or a successor, would almost certainly be strongly anti-Communist, and soon involved in all the problems of a dissident peasantry which undermined Ngo Din Diem and his successors. It would also rely on foreign support, which would undermine its popularity in Vietnam, and arouse the unrelenting hostility of North Vietnam, and the mistrust of China. It would seem only too probable that such a compromise would carry the seeds of further war and revolution. In spite of a flood of propaganda to the contrary, now almost openly recognized as false, there are not two nations in Vietnam, North and South, but one. The urge to unity has been strong among them for at least one hundred years, and was the main force behind opposition to French rule, which partitioned the country. Economically the country is inter-dependent. The northern provinces have the most mineral resources, the heaviest population and the most industry, but lack adequate food production—one reason why Chinese help to North Vietnam has taken in part the form of large shipments of rice.

The southern provinces are a rice bowl, based on the immensely fertile Mekong delta. The natural balance is for the south to supply food to the north and receive the industrial products of the north in exchange. This balance was destroyed by the crystallization of the Geneva cease-fire line into a frontier dividing two hostile governments. Vietnam can never have peace nor prosperity until it is restored. This is well understood by all Vietnamese, northern or southern. The official American propaganda in favour of a divided country to be negotiated at the Paris talks finds little favour with southern Vietnamese, or their leaders, some of whom (like Marshal Ky) are themselves northerners. They make no secret of their hope to reconquer the whole country and crush North Vietnam as well as the National Liberation Front. No nationalist South Vietnamese government could hope to survive or gain real support unless it proclaimed this intention. To claim survival on the basis of foreign protection of a government limited to the south would be to admit ultimate defeat. There can be no lasting peace in Vietnam until the country is reunited, and reunion under a government hostile to China would in itself be an invitation to further disorders.

2. China and Cambodia

The territories of China and of Cambodia, now known as the Khmer Republic, do not adjoin. Between them lies a wide province of northern Laos, and the western part of North Vietnam. In past times the relations between the Chinese empire and this rather distant country were friendly; Cambodia sent envoys to the more powerful Chinese dynasties, which the Chinese emperors, as was their custom, chose to treat as tribute bearing missions. That there were also Chinese return missions is sure, but they are not recorded in great detail by the Chinese records until the mission sent by Khubilai Khan, the Mongol emperor, included on its staff a Chinese scholar named Chou Ta-kuan, who has left the best and most detailed record of the Khmer kingdom with its capital at Angkor. This mission, in the early fourteenth century (1305 A.D.), describes the kingdom and capital as they were on the eve of their decline. In the subsequent centuries the Chinese court concerned itself very little with Cambodia. Ming and Manchu may have chosen to regard it as a tributary country, but relations were slight, and certainly China did nothing to assist Cambodia in her long and losing struggle against invading Thais and Vietnamese. There was some settlement of Chinese in the country—Chou Ta-kuan already reports upon the presence of resident Chinese, whom he implies were former sea rovers, or pirates.

In the middle of the nineteenth century, when the Khmer kingdom was very hard pressed by Vietnamese encroachment and Thai ambition, the arrival of the French, who had just taken control of southern Vietnam, saved the kingdom from extinction. The Cambodians accepted a French Protectorate (1863) and with it, the restricted frontiers which foreign invasions had imposed. They also found that under the French the development of rubber plantations and other estate industries meant a great influx of Vietnamese workers. A large Vietnamese community became resident in Cambodia, but power remained with the French. There was also a considerable Chinese immigration, mainly to the cities, where business opportunities attracted them. The French served to cushion Cambodia against the age old ambitions of her neighbours, Thailand and Vietnam; consequently the French were popular and even welcome in this country. The royal house retained some authority and much respect.

During the Second World War, when French power was weakened by disaster in Europe, the Thais, then in alliance with Japan, made a fresh invasion and seized upon the western provinces, including the ruined site of Angkor. The French could not resist. After the Japanese surrender, the provinces which the Thais had occupied were restored to Cambodia, but the French authority had lost much prestige and credibility. The losing course of the French war in Vietnam portended an end to the Protectorate, and when the Geneva agreements of July 1954 were signed, Cambodia recovered full sovereign independence and the French withdrew. It was at this point that relations between China and the newly freed kingdom were resumed. The Cambodians could feel some obligation towards China, which had been instrumental in bringing about the agreements by which France left Indo-China, but they soon had other problems to trouble them. There was the long lasting quarrel with Thailand, which erupted from time to time in a dispute about the frontiers, which when referred to the Hague Court, was judged favourably to the Cambodian case. Thailand then discontinued diplomatic relations, and the border remained insecure.

The war in Vietnam at this time prevented any resumption of the long standing pressure which former independent Vietnamese regimes had put upon Cambodia. On the other hand the support of America for South Vietnam and the military agreements between Thailand and the U.S.A. were seen with distrust by the Cambodians. The friend of mine enemy is not my friend. Prince Sihanouk, the former King, who gave up the throne first to his father, and on his father's death, to his mother, so that he might devote himself as 'Head of State' to the business of government without being trammelled by ceremony, had proved himself an able and skilful ruler, who was trying to introduce a more modern form of government, and an improved economy. The country was at peace and orderly. The Prince enjoyed the respect, even the reverence of the peasantry, if he did not always command so much devotion among the small administrative and political elites. The problem he had to face was the pressure which the nearby war in Vietnam put upon a weak kingdom with a long jungle frontier which was not too clearly defined and often disregarded by the combatants in Vietnam.

At the Bandung Conference of 1955, only one year after the kingdom had become fully independent, Prince Sihanouk led the Cambodian delegation and there made contact with Chou En-lai, Prime Minister of China, who led the Chinese delegation. The close relationship which developed from this contact reflected the interests of both countries. The Prince became a welcome visitor to Peking, which he visited on several occasions. China not only recognized Cambodia, but approved the policy of neutrality which was the keystone of Sihanouk's political standpoint. It may seem strange that the leaders of a Communist Party and government, such as Mao Tse-tung and Chou En-lai should establish close and friendly relations with a regime presided over by a king—or former king—of ancient lineage who in his subjects' eyes was virtually divine. Ideology hardly entered into the question. There was, in northern Cambodia, a small 'Red Khmer' movement which had arisen, with the support of the Vietnamese Communist Party, in the last days of French rule. It did not flourish under the independent kingdom and was proscribed. It soon became insignificant and virtually faded away. No doubt it was no longer the policy of the Vietnamese Communists to give it support, and it was certainly not in Chinese interests to do so. Cambodia was neutral. This meant in practice that the Cambodian government refused to join in the Vietnamese War, or permit American military activity in the country, and would have no American base set up within its borders. It was much more difficult to prevent Vietnamese Communist forces from retreating, when pressed, across the jungle frontier, resting, and then returning to their own country. This question continued to be a source of dispute between the Cambodian government and the U.S.A. for several years. On the other hand the Vietnamese Communists did not penetrate beyond a very few miles inside the border, they avoided occupying any town or villages and they were at pains to conceal their presence as much as possible.

China developed a plan of aid to Cambodia, partly to replace American aid programmes which had been discontinued. Roads, airports, and other constructions were built by Chinese aid. Cambodia, trying to be neutral, also accepted aid from countries of the non-Communist world other than America. The fact that the two neighbours of Cambodia, South Vietnam and Thailand were both allies of America and also traditional and much distrusted enemies of Cambodia, was the reason why Prince Sihanouk's neutrality tended to be somewhat more tolerant of the Communist side than of the American side in the Vietnam War. Moreover Sihanouk believed that in the long run the Americans could not win the war, that Vietnam would be reunited under a Communist government, and that the real interests of Cambodia were therefore best served by friendship with China which would in the end be the only power able to restrain Vietnamese pressure upon his country. There is as yet nothing to show that this assessment was wrong. He saw clearly that to commit the country to the war on either of the two sides would open it to invasion and devastation. This is what has happened since his successors abandoned his policy.

For China, the neutrality of Cambodia was desirable, indeed better than an open commitment to the Communist side. That would have justified an American invasion and the spread of the war to Cambodia. There was from the Chinese and Vietnamese Communist point of view no benefit to be derived from such action. The routes by which supplies to South Vietnam were brought passed, in part, through Cambodia's wild northern provinces, and also used the port of Sihanoukville, recently developed on the short Cambodian sea coast. The land routes could not be extensively bombed as they were through a neutral country, and the port could not be blockaded for the same reason. There is no provision of international law which prevents a neutral country from trading with belligerents, nor forces it to close its communications to their goods. Neutrality therefore suited the Vietnamese Communists and therefore also China. The interest of China in the Cambodian question largely, if not entirely, turned upon the degree with which that country was involved in the Vietnam War. From the Chinese standpoint, the less the better, so as to deny the Americans any cause for spreading the conflict into Cambodia. The Vietnamese Communists, on the other hand had another concern, the advantages of having frontier districts of Cambodia available to them as areas in which they could rest and supply their forces. It is still very disputable whether the Vietnamese Communists had expanded this intrusion in any significant way in 1969. The attempts to prove that large installations were located in the frontier districts did not succeed when the Americans, having invaded the region, failed to find any such major camps and headquarters as were alleged to be there.

The situation in which China extended friendship and recognition to Cambodia, Cambodia tried to maintain neutrality, and the Vietnamese Communists made use of the frontier districts, continued for several years at least after major American participation in the Vietmanese War. There seems no reason why it should not have continued until the American withdrawal would probably have removed the need for the Vietnamese Communists to use these areas.

The overthrow of Prince Sihanouk's government by a military coup when he was abroad in March 1970 altered the situation fundamentally. An American and South Vietnamese invasion followed, and although it was promised that American forces would leave Cambodia by the end of June 1970, the Saigon government made no such promise and did not withdraw. The war spread into Cambodia, with much devastation. Prince Sihanouk, taking refuge in Peking, has there set up a government in exile, which has been recognized by China, but not yet by Soviet Russia. The Chinese have therefore committed themselves to the support of Sihanouk's party, which is stronger in the countryside than that of his enemies. It has been clear that some of the forces opposing the South Vietnamese invaders have been Cambodian followers of Sihanouk. It seems very possible that he can retain, or recover, full control of the northern part of the country, and far from impossible that he may be restored to full power. If that comes about, he will owe his restored fortunes to China and to the Vietnamese Communists, and with war in the country, neutrality will be impossible.

3. China and Laos

The territory of Laos borders on China's southwestern province of Yünnan, but the region is mountainous and jungle covered and there are no modern communications across the relatively short frontier between the two countries. The easy road of access between China and Laos is through North Vietnam. In earlier times the principalities into which Laos was divided either were subject to the Cambodian empire or, later, came under the suzerainty of either Thailand or the Vietnamese empire ruled from Hanoi. There is therefore no long standing direct connection between China and Laos. Following the French occupation of Vietnam and the declaration of a protectorate over Cambodia, Laos also came under French rule. It was not a unified country, the three major principalities, in the north, centre and south of the country were virtually separately administered, and the royal enclave of the king at his capital, Luang Prabang, not far from the French administrative capital at Vientiane, made a fourth state. Under French rule Laos had no international identity and consequently no relations with China. Some Chinese migration to the larger cities followed the economic development undertaken by the French.

After the Geneva Agreements of 1954 Laos became an independent state, but it was far from being a consolidated country. The three great principalities continued in almost total independence of each other, and the most northerly was infiltrated by the North Vietnamese forces, who there encouraged the formation of a Communist movement, the Pathet Lao or Free Laotian movement. This was headed by Prince Souvannavong who was a half brother of the Prince Souvanna Phouma who ruled the centre area and was acknowledged as the Prime Minister of the state. Internal politics took on a flavour of modern terminology while remaining essentially feudal. A sporadic civil war between the Pathet Lao and the central regime continued for several years, and as it became clear that Vietnamese influence was increasing, and Laos was becoming involved in the Vietnamese War, an attempt was made to impose peace and neutrality upon the country.

In 1962 an international conference, attended both by the U.S.A. and by China, reached an agreement for the neutralization of the country. The next year the escalation of the Vietnamese war and the bombing of North Vietnam led to the increased use of Laotian territory by the North Vietnamese for supplying their forces and the National Liberation Front in South Vietnam. This was the 'Ho Chi Minh trail', a complex of jungle roads leading from North Vietnam through eastern Laos to the South Vietnamese border with Laos. To secure this route the Pathet Lao were encouraged to retain control of the northern provinces of Laos. U.S. intervention, largely clandestine, through a military mission in Vientiane, was the response, and the Ho Chi Minh trail was bombed continuously from that time onwards. The hope of a neutral Laos faded away, the civil war continued, and a number of military coups and violent changes of regime occurred in the non-Communist part of the country.

The main influence on the Communist side was exercised by North Vietnam for which the country and its routes to the south was of high strategic importance. China, as the ally and friend of the Communist regime in Vietnam, seems to have contributed road making experts, engineers and, later, formations of road building units not only for the improvement of communications between North Vietnam and Laos, but also to open better communications between northern Laos and the Chinese province of Yünnan. The two sides in the Laotian civil war continued in conflict, punctuated by abortive truces, but in 1969, the Pathet Lao made significant gains of territory, probably in order to counter the U.S. bombing of the roads to the east.

There are two aspects of the Laotian situation which are not often made plain. Firstly, the country is ethnically divided between the Laotian people who occupy the valleys and rice growing lowlands along the Mekong river; and the hill tribes, the Meo, who occupy the higher mountains. This situation resembles that in neighbouring Chinese Yunnan, where a similar division exists, the position being complicated, as in Laos, by the fact that the higher hills occupied by Meo (in China by Miao, the same people) are often isolated by lowlands occupied by Laotians, thus making a vertical rather than a horizontal division of races. Meo tend to be hostile to all lowlanders, no matter what their political allegiance and consequently, in government controlled provinces, take the Communist side, and in Pathet Lao areas, are inclined to favour the government. Their attitude is determined by the age old hostility between mountaineer and lowland farmer, not by politics. It is thus very difficult to impose any peace upon this country, and equally easy to stir up revolts and disturbances.

The second peculiar factor in Laotian affairs is the importance of the opium trade. Opium is best grown at an altitude between 2,000 and 4,000 feet; above these altitudes the crop is poorer and subject to frost risk. This makes the low hill country bordering upon Chinese Yunnan (which is much higher) the ideal area for the production of the opium poppy. Northern Laos, eastern Thailand and the Shan states of Burma provide this climate, and it is in these regions that opium cultivation is very profitable, and also the main economic resource of the mountain dwellers, whose production of rice is insufficient, and who have no other valuable cash crop to raise. The control of the opium on its route to the markets in the great seaboard cities of eastern Asia is a prize for which local military rulers have long contended. When opium was grown in western China, before the Communist regime came to power, the control of the traffic was a major political-military factor in the constant local civil wars. So it continues to be in the borderlands south and west of China. It is, naturally, being an illegal traffic, not a well documented story, and largely escapes publicity, but it remains a powerful factor in the alternating wars and truces between rival factions in the borderlands of all these countries.

China's relations with Laos, which hardly existed until the French withdrew, turn upon the degree to which Laos is involved in the Vietnamese War. China was in favour of the neutralization of Laos in 1964, because that proposal promised to take Laos out of the conflict. The establishment of a pro-U.S. government which might admit American air bases to the northern provinces of Laos, ad- ᵗ'journing China, would be contrary to Chinese interests. Therefore, aid to the Pathet Lao to control this region and if possible expand it, is to the interest of China. Since the bombing of North Vietnam was discontinued, American bombing of the Ho Chi Minh trail and other Pathet Lao held areas of Laos intensified, and this must be closely related to the increased activity by Pathet Lao against the government held regions in which American air personnel associated with the bombing raids were active.

After the revolution against Prince Sihanouk and the American-South Vietnamese invasion of Cambodia, when China had made it clear that she remained a supporter of Prince Sihanouk, a new alliance of North Vietnam, Pathet Lao, and the National Liberation Front was formed in support of Prince Sihanouk's government in exile, located in Peking. This movement clearly had full Chinese support. The Cambodian invasion widened the Vietnamese War into one which at once involved all the countries of the old French Indo-China. Southern as well as northern Laos had become the scene of military operations and the conflict continued to spread. It must be expected that as long as the war continues in Cambodia, China, like North Vietnam, will be concerned to sustain the Pathet Lao and will not accept any solution to the troubles of Laos that puts China herself, and North Vietnam, at a strategic disadvantage. Chinese relations with Laos are a product of the Vietnamese War, and must be expected to continue on the same lines as long as that war lasts.

Chapter Two

CHINA AND INDONESIA

Chinese relations with the countries of the East Indian Archipelago, the modern Indonesia, date back many centuries. They were on the whole friendly, being either religious, through pilgrims on their way to India, or commercial. Only at infrequent intervals did any Chinese dynasty make direct political or military interventions in the affairs of the various kingdoms among which the islands were divided. The last occasion was the succession of maritime expeditions, mainly engaged in official trade, sent out by the Ming Emperor Yung Lo in the early years of the fifteenth century. When these were discontinued by his successors, official relations declined, and with the coming of the Dutch, Indonesia gradually lost independence and became a colonial territory.

During the colonial period of Dutch rule China could have no relations with Indonesia other than commercial, but the period saw a great increase in the immigrant Chinese community. This had been established in some parts of the archipelago for many centuries, as early as the thirteenth century in Sumatra, and although very little is known of these settlements after the Ming expeditions, it is probable that they continued to exist. Chinese immigration in the Dutch period continued, and a considerable portion of the resident Chinese population in Indonesia at the time of independence had had roots in the country for upwards of three centuries. On the other hand, although long established, the Chinese community was small in comparison with the large Javanese population and with the lesser, but still considerable, native population in the other islands. Much of the migration occurred in the nineteenth century, especially in the second half of that period. Early in the twentieth century an estimate of one million Chinese was accepted by the Dutch authorities. At the time of independence the Chinese population was estimated to be two and one half million, of which over 70 per cent were born in the country. The Javanese and other races in the islands at that time were estimated to number about eighty million.

During the Japanese occupation of Indonesia in the Second World War the Chinese community found itself in a difficult position. China was at war with Japan, and thus in a sense an ally of the Dutch. The Chinese community as a whole sympathized with and had given financial support to the motherland. On the other hand the Indonesian population and its leaders, later to be the founders of the Indonesian Republic, were hostile to Dutch colonial rule and willing to collaborate to some degree with the Japanese. This attitude tended to create, or to exacerbate, anti-Chinese feeling among the Indonesian people.

The Indonesian nationalist movement was making rapid progress towards assumption of control of the country during the final stages of the war; shortly after the Japanese surrender, Sukarno and Hatta declared Indonesia's independence of the Netherlands. Allied forces which were landed to take the surrender of the Japanese army of occupation and to repatriate it to Japan did not recognize this act, but equally did not attempt to suppress the nationalist movement, for which task, indeed, their numbers were quite inadequate. The Dutch returned, at least to the main ports, and refused to accept the declaration of independence. Negotiations for a new status for the whole of the Dutch colonial empire, punctuated by 'police actions' in 1947 and 1948 in which the Dutch attempted to suppress the Republic of Indonesia, then established in the interior of Java, led in 1949 to international recognition of the Republic and the end of Dutch rule. It was only at this point that China could establish relations with the new state.

Immediately after the Second World War, during the Indonesian struggle with the Dutch, China was still under the government of the Kuomintang, or Nationalist Party, headed by General Chiang Kai-shek. But he was soon involved in the civil war which ended in 1949 in his defeat and the expulsion of his Party and followers from the mainland of China, to take refuge in the island of Taiwan. The People's Republic of China, declared at Peking on 1 October 1949 was thus almost exactly contemporary with the official recognition of the Indonesian Republic. The Nationalist regime had had little time or opportunity to devise any new policy to meet the changed status of Indonesia; relations between the two countries since the Second World War are thus essentially those between the Communist regime in China, and the nationalist regime of the Republic of Indonesia.

These relations have been governed by two factors. Firstly, until 1965, there were the sympathy and fellow feeling shared by both countries as opponents of colonialism and, to varying degrees, of the Western Powers. President Sukarno during his term of power never refrained from making his attitude to colonialism and to what he called imperialism very plain. China shared these views. Mutual recognition and diplomatic relations had been established at an early date following the victory of both parties in their respective countries. Indonesia was for long one of the most favoured of foreign non-Communist states in Chinese eyes.

The second, more troublesome question, was the presence in Indonesia of a large resident Chinese community who were mainly engaged in commerce, industry and small scale trading. They were thus a capitalist community in the view of the Chinese Communists, but they were also a Chinese community. To the Indonesians they were alien and unwelcome. In spite of the long residence and local descent of a large part of the community, their predominance in trade, industry and the professions made them the object of envy and dislike. The fact that, although put under many restrictions during Dutch rule, the Chinese had nonetheless on the whole profited from the colonial regime and become a wealthy class made them favour the Dutch rather than the nationalist revolutionaries. Most businessmen unless very definitely committed to a political standpoint prefer stability to the risk of disorder and confusion. The Dutch imposed stability, the Republic, still uncertain and threatened by its own internal dissensions, seemed a dangerous alternative to many Chinese businessmen. Thus the new regime considered the Chinese community hostile to their own revolution.

During the first few years of the Republic of Indonesia there were no significant developments in Sino-Indonesian relations. The Republic was much preoccupied with internal problems; the Chinese had first the Korean War on their hands, and then the Vietnamese crisis which was temporarily resolved at the Geneva Conference of 1954. It was not until the following year, 1955, that the calling of a conference of Asian nations at Bandung in Indonesia gave scope for important new initiatives which concerned not only interstate relations but also the thorny question of the Chinese community in Indonesia.

The nature of this problem must be examined before it is possible to consider the solutions which were proposed. Chinese immigration into Indonesia preceded Dutch rule by several centuries, but had not then been on a very large scale. After the Dutch became established in the islands, Chinese immigration increased and was in strong demand to supply labour for estate agriculture. In the second half of the nineteenth century the Chinese tended to move into the outer islands. In the west of Borneo, they had been established since the middle of the eighteenth century. At the end of the Second World War the Chinese population may have attained about two and a half millions. They were divided both by their origin and their place of settlement. About 70 per cent were descendants of earlier immigrants, many with mixed blood; some families had been in the country for three hundred years, perhaps longer. But nearly 30 per cent were recent immigrants, born in China. The latter were known as Sinkheh, a word which is the southern dialect version of Standard Chinese 'Hsin K'e', meaning 'new guest' or 'immigrant'. As such it is widely used over all Southeast Asia. The long established families were known to the Indonesians as Peranakans. These formed the majority in Java and in Borneo, but the newcomers were in a majority in the outer islands including Sumatra.

The Chinese community was also divided by its local origin in China, which being in all cases from the southeastern provinces, the 'dialect belt' of China, meant that they spoke many differing dialects, which tended to mark off the community into sharply separated segments. Java and many of the eastern islands beyond it were settled by Hokkien speakers, coming from the district of the port of Amoy in southern Fukien province, on the southeast coast of China. Hokkien is their way of pronouncing the name of the province, Fukien (in northern standard speech Fuchien). The community in Borneo is predominantly Hakka, a group descended from refugees who in the twelfth and thirteenth centuries fled to the south of China before the Tartar invasions of that epoch. They settled in Kuangtung and in Fukien and Kuangsi provinces, but have remained a rather underprivileged group in those regions, since the better land was already in the hands of earlier settlers and natives. The Hakka became, for economic reasons, a migrant people, who have settled widely in many parts of Southeast Asia. They came in strength to Borneo as long ago as the mid eighteenth century, almost a hundred years before Dutch authority was enforced in the island, and set up a curious social and political organization called kongsi (in standard Chinese kungssu) which is the word which has today been used to render the modern term 'company' in Chinese. The Hakka kongsi in Borneo were groups who obtained from the local sultan rights to open mines or settle on uncultivated land. They in effect ruled themselves, by their customary laws, and were hardly at all controlled or oppressed by the sultans, who were content to receive a tribute or revenue from the kongsi. The development of this quasi-republican form of government among the Borneo Hakka is a curious aspect of overseas Chinese life, in no way deriving from experience or practice in the homeland at that time. It illustrates the manner in which migrant groups in a strange and new environment will create social institutions of their own, adapted to their new circumstances.

When the Dutch established direct administration in Borneo in the nineteenth century they clashed with the Hakka kongsi, and ultimately, after a long struggle, suppressed them. The Hakka community, however, survived, and revived, remaining the dominant group of Chinese migrants in Borneo, for which country they supplied the majority of skilled labour and small scale commerce.

Hakka also settled, rather later, in Sumatra, but in that island there were also large numbers of another dialect group, the Teochiu, from the neighbourhood of Chaochou and its port of Swatow, in northern Kuangtung, across the border from Fukien. 'Teochiu' is the local pronunciation of 'Chaochou'. The Teochiu, like their competitors from Amoy and the Hakkas, were not a privileged people in China. Their region was remote from the capital, and they produced relatively few scholars to enter the civil service. They carried very little political influence in Peking. For these reasons, and the overcrowding of the population in the restricted areas of fertile rice land on a mountainous coast, they had long been a migrant folk, who are found in many parts of Southeast Asia, especially in Thailand.

Finally the Cantonese, another migrant people, but one with close connections with the greatest and most civilized city of south China, Canton, were found in most or indeed in all parts of Indonesia, where they tended to occupy a higher economic status than other migrant groups attained. Industry and mining, finance, the professions and larger scale commerce were the Cantonese preserve, though not exclusive to them.

Another aspect of the Chinese community of all origins was that until rather late, from 1920 onwards, men greatly outnumbered women. This had led to much intermarriage with Indonesians, but the children were always reckoned to be Chinese. In fact a large percentage of the Peranakans had Indonesian blood. It was only after the fall of the Manchu dynasty that the free and increasing migration of Chinese women to Southeast Asia began to influence the character of the community, and no doubt, to emphasize its alien character. The Chinese were tenacious of their culture and national traditions and customs. They established Chinese language schools, and after the Republic came in in China, these were often staffed with teachers recruited in China, and used Chinese textbooks with a curriculum modelled on the educational system of China. These characteristics were tolerated by the Dutch, but were unwelcome to the Indonesian nationalists.

The Chinese domination in the fields of commerce and petty shop-keeping throughout the country, and in market gardening near large towns and cities, as also in many of the professions and in industry, was a further source of friction. The Dutch had been content to let the Chinese community take over these occupations because Indonesians were rarely equipped for them, and because the growth of an intellectual and commercial élite of wealthy Chinese was in itself a barrier to the equivalent development of these classes among the Indonesians. The Dutch saw the Chinese to some degree as a buffer between themselves and Indonesian nationalist aspirations. They firmly excluded the Chinese from any part in political or administrative life, but did nothing to hinder their acquisition of skills, knowledge and riches. Indonesians of the middle class tended to feel very strongly that the Chinese community was parasitic upon the Dutch and kept Indonesians out of their due place in their own country. There was considerable ill-feeling against the Chinese; there was also the fact that the small Chinese shop-keeper in the countryside was usually also the money lender, and the Indonesian peasantry was often deeply in his debt. The role of the Chinese in many ways resembled that of the Jews in nineteenth century Europe—disliked by the natives, but patronized and used by the ruling class; in Indonesia the latter were the Dutch.

After the independence of Indonesia, the Indonesian Republic passed laws restricting the activities of the Chinese, and in other ways discriminating against them. In 1946 laws defining the citizenship status of Chinese virtually excluded all those not born in Indonesia, and hemmed in those that had been with many restrictions. In 1950 one year after independence was finally recognized, all Chinese immigration was forbidden. This prohibition has remained in force and the Chinese in the Indonesian Republic have received no significant or even measurable increase in numbers from immigration from that time.

These measures did not in themselves solve the problems of nationality and citizenship. The Chinese Nationalist regime, which had only just been driven out of power, had for many years based its policy towards overseas Chinese on the legal maxim, *jus sanguinis,* the identification of a man's nationality by his descent. All Chinese, whether they were born in China or not, were regarded as Chinese citizens, and even if they held another nationality by right of birth or passport, they still could claim, at will, to be Chinese and be acknowledged by the Chinese government as such. 'Once a Chinese, always a Chinese' was the popular definition of this status, and it must be recognized that it was far from unwelcome to the great mass of the overseas Chinese.

The Kuomintang (Nationalist Party) in China had good reasons for extending favours to the overseas Chinese. Firstly, the Manchu dynasty had neglected their interests and even, for many years, regarded them as a subversive element which was hostile to their dynasty. So the Nationalists and their Republican predecessors favoured the overseas Chinese. Secondly they had found in these communities a never failing source of strong financial support for the revolution, and after that, for the Nationalist Party itself. Thirdly the Chinese overseas remitted a steady and in aggregate large fund of foreign exchange for the support of their family relatives at home. This came, naturally, mainly from the Sinkheh, the new immigrants to Southeast Asia, whose families still remained in the ancestral village. Up to the end of the war the allegiance of the great majority of the Indonesian Chinese to Nationalist China was not in doubt. Until the Japanese occupation they had contributed money for the Chinese national resistance. The Dutch had never encouraged them to become citizens of their colonial empire, still less, to take up Dutch nationality. The Japanese occupation broke these links for the time being, and within a very few years of the Japanese surrender in 1945, the Nationalist government was overthrown in China (1949). China, the Indonesian Chinese, and the new Indonesian Republican nationalists were all alike faced with a totally new situation.

It was only after the Korean War had been ended in a prolonged armistice which acknowledged a military stalemate, that the new power of Communist China became evident to the other peoples of Southeast Asia and their rulers. This was no longer the weak and distracted China of the Kuomintang, nor the effete empire of the Manchus; this was a new—or rather a very old, and mainly forgotten, phenomenon—a strong China, which had an interest and might develop a policy towards the countries of Southeast Asia and their Chinese communities. Indonesia had recognized the People's Republic of China (the Communist regime) and that government had in turn recognized the Indonesian Republic. There was thus no obstacle to a new approach to the problem of the Chinese resident community, and some prospect of successful negotiations.

It was not until the latter part of 1954, four years and more after the independence of Indonesia and the establishment of the People's Republic of China, that the two powers began to negotiate concerning the most serious problem which they had in common. Indonesia had been preoccupied with much internal unrest and insecurity; China had had the Korean War, and then the Vietnam settlement of 1954 to preoccupy her. But late in 1954 negotiations were opened in Peking on the problem of dual citizenship, the situation in which

Indonesian Chinese were both citizens of China, and also, in some cases, of Indonesia. When the Bandung Conference of Asian Nations was called in Djakarta in April 1955 the negotiations were transferred to Djakarta, and were carried on to a conclusion, the Agreement being signed on 22 April 1955. Indonesia was the only Southeast Asian country to attempt to solve these problems by negotiation.

The main provisions of this agreement, which was not ratified for several years owing to the objections of various Indonesian political parties, were that China renounced the Chinese Nationalist doctrine of the *jus sanguinis* ('once a Chinese always a Chinese') and agreed that all Chinese born in Indonesia should have the right to choose their nationality within a time limit of two years. Those who chose Indonesian nationality would then become full Indonesian citizens; those who preferred to choose Chinese nationality would from that time onward be aliens in Indonesia, and could be refused residence permits. China undertook to accept such citizens back in the home country.

The Chinese Prime Minister, Chou En-lai, who was the chief negotiator for China, also announced in public at the Bandung Conference that any other Asian nation with a resident Chinese minority community was welcome to conclude a similar agreement with the People's Republic, the only condition being that they must recognize the People's Republic as the sole legitimate government of China. No other Asian nation took up this offer. Of those with large Chinese minorities, Malaya had not yet attained independence, nor had Singapore. Vietnam was divided and in confusion. The Philippine Republic was ruled by a strongly anti-Communist oligarchy which was also anti-Chinese of all kinds; and Burma, although in diplomatic relations with China, was not very much interested in this issue as the Chinese minority was small and was also long established. Thailand, with a very large Chinese community, was opposed to the Peking government, and also pursued anti-Chinese policies at home. It may well be that some of these nations now regret that they could not, or did not, take advantage of a mood in Chinese foreign policy more moderate than some which have followed.

Indonesia did not at once ratify this agreement. There were strong hostile pressures among the political parties, particularly in the Muslim parties. They wanted first to pass a series of laws restraining Chinese activities and imposing further restrictions on Chinese before they could acquire citizenship. These ideas were finally embodied in legislation enacted in 1958, by which not only all migrants born abroad, but also their children born in Indonesia were debarred from ever becoming Indonesian citizens, while those born in the country had also to be descended from fathers born in Indonesia to be eligible to take the option to become Indonesian citizens. In addition a number of measures restricted the activities of all Chinese, whether citizens or not. The Chinese press, with one or two rare (and carefully controlled) exceptions was banned. Almost all Chinese language schools were closed except for aliens. An aliens tax was imposed on those Chinese who could not qualify for citizenship. All remittances to families in China were stopped. Foreign exchange to Chinese firms was limited unless it could be shown that the firm was at least 50 per cent Indonesian owned. Import licences to Chinese firms were restricted, and Chinese were forbidden to hold shares in rice mills. All these measures struck at the customs, culture and traditional occupations of the Chinese community. The provision that Indonesian ownership of 50 per cent must be interpreted as meaning the exclusion of Chinese Indonesian citizens, made it clear that even those who opted for Indonesian citizenship would still suffer discrimination.

In effect the act of 1958 made many of the provisions of the Agreement of 1955 rather meaningless; and restored, or maintained, the situation in which the Chinese community had been placed (in Republican territory) since 1946. It was estimated that about 50 per cent of those Chinese who had the choice decided to renounce Chinese citizenship, and opt for Indonesian nationality. This proportion covered most of the established settlers whose families had been in the country for several centuries, or at least two or three generations. A very large number, including all the migrants who might have been in Indonesia most of their lives, now became aliens. In 1958 the rather small number of resident Chinese who neither could become Indonesian citizens nor wished to opt for citizenship of the Peoples' Republic, preferring the Nationalist regime in Taiwan (with which Indonesia had no relations) were harassed and in effect driven from the country. Neither Peking nor Djakarta regarded them as covered by the provisions of the Bandung Agreement. In 1959 it was the Chinese who carried on the rural village trade of the country who struck opposition. They were forbidden to continue trading and were driven away to the cities. A certain amount of violence, some killings and pillage accompanied this harsh treatment. In 1960 in spite of the friction which these policies had caused, the Indonesian parliament ratified the Bandung Agreement, having successfully rendered its spirit, if not its letter, largely inoperative.

It was estimated that the Chinese community in 1960 was approximately two and one half million people. Of these rather more than 70 per cent were born in Indonesia. They were more concentrated, and formed the majority of the Chinese community, in Java and in

Borneo. Immigrants formed the majority in Sumatra and the eastern islands. It has been estimated that between 150,000 and 300,000 people were directly affected by the laws confiscating rural trading establishments and the laws restricting other Chinese occupations. No compensation was paid to these deprived people, many of whom had to live on charity in the cities, or seek as much work as they could find. China was thus faced with a very real problem. On the one hand, the Chinese government wished to maintain friendly relations with President Sukarno's government which in international affairs followed policies which China supported. On the other hand the persecution of the large Indonesian Chinese community, in spite of the Agreement of Bandung, aroused strong resentments. The Indonesian government had tried to use the first factor to mitigate the second. In October 1959 the Foreign Minister, Dr Subandrio, who was later well known as a strongly hostile critic of the Western capitalist world, claimed to the Chinese that the Chinese in Indonesia were capitalists and monopolists who deserved no sympathy from a Communist government. The Chinese did not accept this excuse.

Foreign Minister Ch'en Yi replied that the mass of the Chinese, the overwhelming majority of the community, were 'working people', and neither 'colonialists' nor a monopoly group. As such they should not be made a target for discrimination, and they should receive fair compensation for their losses. He also offered to assist in the repatriation of those who, having lost their livelihood in Indonesia, wished to go to China. Some repatriation, but in effect very little, and on a wholly inadequate scale, was carried out in late 1960 and in 1961. Ch'en Yi visited Indonesia in April 1961, mainly to sign with Indonesia a Treaty of Friendship which was intended to further the larger aim of Chinese policy, to win Indonesia to her side in international relations and in opposition to the Western powers. In practice China confined her protests about the treatment of Chinese in Indonesia to words; it can be argued that there was little she could do about it had she decided that words were not sufficient. The attempt to gain more just treatment for the Chinese through the Agreement of Bandung had not truly achieved very much, but the significance of that instrument should not, nonetheless, be discounted.

By renouncing the long established claim of the Chinese Nationalists that all overseas Chinese came under *jus sanguinis,* and were Chinese citizens by birth, the Chinese Communist regime had reversed a policy which had been very much disliked and even feared by both the former colonial regimes in Southeast Asia and by the independent states which had succeeded, or were now succeeding to their authority. The British rulers of Malaya had actually declared the local branches of the Kuomintang, then the ruling party in China, to be subversive organizations, and had closed them in the years before the war. The participation of Chinese in political life and in general their acceptability as citizens in all these countries was hindered and harmed by a doctrine which seemed to diminish their loyalty to the lands of their residence, and continue to use them for China's national designs and policies. Fund raising for the Kuomintang, and for anti-Japanese defence in the 1930s had caused some embarrassments for weakened neutral colonial regimes trying to keep out of China's quarrels and fearful of Japanese ambition. Peking now officially renounced these policies and attitudes. It was asserted that for those overseas Chinese who wished to return to the home country there was a warm welcome and ample opportunities for employment in the 'service of the people'. China wanted the skills of her overseas sons. Those who had made their homes abroad, and did not wish to return, should accept the responsibilities of their decision, become citizens, and renounce Chinese allegiance. In turn, they should not be discriminated against on account of ethnic origin.

Had China not been also a Communist state these policies would have met with a much warmer response. But many people in Southeast Asia, and elsewhere, had their doubts; they feared that the new strong China would continue to exercise an attraction upon the loyalties and sentiments of the Chinese communities, perhaps a greater attraction than the weak Kuomintang had been able to attain. They feared a 'fifth column', and they also feared that Communist ideas, now become national and almost official to the Chinese abroad, would thereby penetrate among the native population also. It is very difficult to say whether these fears have been justified, in part, or at all. It is equally difficult to say that they are wholly groundless. If the Malayan Communist Party was mainly recruited from the Chinese population, the Indonesian Communist Party—far larger and for long much more influential—was just as overwhelmingly Indonesian in composition and incidentally much older, as a party, than the Chinese Communist Party itself. In most of the countries concerned, Communist parties, where they were at all significant, were native, not Chinese in membership. Chinese in the vast majority avoided any overt political allegiance. The evidence of a 'fifth column' is simply not to be found. The evidence that China has continued to attract the interest, and often the devotion, of the younger generation is clear and strong. But the evidence that the Peking government has tried to use its overseas Chinese connections to cause trouble in these countries is inconclusive, and mainly negative.

On the other hand the Bandung Agreement of 1955 remains in force; it is a model which China has offered to the other countries having large or small Chinese communities, and it continues to provide the only workable system of relations between China and those countries, when events and changes gradually compel them to recognize China and enter into relations with Peking. That this must come, everyone now knows. China will not disappear; she grows stronger, and must under any circumstances play a major part in East Asia. Sooner or later all must deal with her, and largely, on her own terms. The terms for coping with the Chinese community problem have been made clear in the Bandung Agreement and it is not likely that they will be repudiated or altered. They have made it difficult for opponents to sustain the charge that China seeks more than natural justice for her ethnic related former citizens abroad, or for those who still retain Chinese nationality. The justification for discrimination and suspicion of the Chinese provided by the Nationalist law of *jus sanguinis* has been removed. In the long run this change must have profound effects upon the relations between China and her southern neighbours, and upon the situation of the overseas Chinese themselves. As time passes and the immigrant population, no longer swollen by newcomers, merges with those who were born in the country, the argument that the Chinese are aliens must also lose its force. The world has many examples of peoples descended from migrant communities who have either formed new nations or integrated with their hosts. It will not be possible to claim that this evolution must exclude Chinese.

On the other hand the Peking government, in its relations with Indonesia, carefully refrained from using any racial argument in favour of the Chinese community. The Indonesian Chinese, said Ch'en Yi, are 'working people'—not 'my fellow countrymen'. China would not claim that 'bourgeois' Chinese must be protected by a Communist regime just because they too were Chinese; but the Chinese, of any social origin, who returned to China were welcomed as returning natives prepared to accept the changed social system of their home land. There is, in fact not a little evidence to show that 'bourgeois' Chinese returning to China from Indonesia and elsewhere did not fit very well into the home system. They may have had skills, but not always the skills the home government sought or wished to use. The rather half-hearted steps taken to repatriate the Chinese driven from the Indonesian countryside may well be connected with this fact. A very large number of Chinese small traders, mainly returning to one province (Fukien) could be a serious problem for the local authorities, and not one easily passed on to the country at large.

The record of the Chinese People's Republic's relations with Indonesia hardly bears out the fears of those who detect danger in every policy that government pursues. In respect of the treatment of the Chinese community, China was not in practice able to do much to alleviate their hardship nor to mitigate the discrimination against them. Even the repatriation programme was largely ineffective, and after the worsening of Sino-Indonesian relations virtually came to an end. The Agreement of Bandung gave the Chinese residents no better status than they had had since the independence of the Republic, and in fact the Act of 1958 derogated from that status by making only those whose fathers as well as themselves had been born in the country eligible to choose Indonesian nationality. China's renunciation of the *jus sanguinis*, finally ratified in 1960, may prove a long-term advantage for China, but it did little or nothing for the Chinese now living in Indonesia. Those who believe that all Communist parties pursue common objectives must consider the Indonesian case; the Communist Party (P.K.I.) was among the strongest of the political forces in the Republic. If it was at one with the Chinese Communist Party on all aspects of policy it could have used its very great influence with President Sukarno to further the aims of the Chinese government in respect of the resident Chinese, which were to cool off the antagonism felt towards that community by the Indonesian people, to facilitate the repatriation of those wishing to leave the country, and to alleviate the lot of those who decided to remain. There is evidence that the P.K.I. did resist anti-Chinese actions, with the consequence that its political enemies were able later to label it as pro-Chinese; but in spite of this it was an entirely Indonesian orientated party and did not support the interests of China.

It cannot truly be said that China was much more successful in her other policy towards Indonesia, that of winning the friendship of the government and forging a strong tie between the two countries in opposition to the Western powers. After the Treaty of Friendship of 1961 the Chinese government seems to have been ready to sacrifice the interests of the Chinese community, for which it could do little, in order to maintain good relations with President Sukarno's government, which was moving into a position of outright hostility to the Western powers. Verbal support was given to the policies of the President in West Irian, and in the larger issue of 'confrontation' with Malaysia. But in the latter, at least, the Chinese policy was rather cautious. It may be wondered whether China was really very anxious to see the regime in Singapore and in Kuala Lumpur overthrown in favour of others which might have been as strongly motivated by racial antagonism to the resident Chinese as the Indonesian parties were. In any case there was little positive or practical aid which China could give, even if so inclined. Indonesia obtained her war materials largely from Russia, and what China had to spare was before long needed to assist North Vietnam and the National Liberation Front of South Vietnam in their struggle with the Diem government and its U.S. backers. This was clearly a contest of vital importance to Chinese national interests, and a full scale struggle, whereas the confrontation with Malaysia was concerned with a problem in which China's interest was not so obviously involved, nor so clearly defined. Moreover it was not really a war at all; it was a series of skirmishes and small raids, almost wholly ineffective, and never pressed with true determination. These are not the kinds of operations which fitted with the tradition of revolutionary war evolved in China itself, and it may be surmised that they did not greatly impress Chinese policy makers. China was not committed by a military alliance to Indonesia, and as a war with Britain, the protector of Malaysia, was certainly not in China's interests and could only have far reaching and disastrous consequences, China had no incentive to make any open showing of support in a practical manner.

It may be that there was some disillusion on both sides as the results of confrontation continued to be meagre. There was much apprehension in the Western world that the movement of power within Indonesia was tending to greater Communist influence over the President, and that a Communist participation in the government, which would develop into a major force, and then result in the total takeover by the Communist Party, was in prospect. It cannot be known how far the Chinese anticipated the same result, nor whether they saw it as entirely desirable. On the international front, in the balance of power between Communist and non-Communist states, such a result would have been a large gain. Much of Southeast Asia would be then dominated by Communist governments. But there were also risks. That of foreign intervention could not be discounted. The Communist Party in Indonesia might be opposed, and the opponents might be induced to call for U.S. support. Before the escalation of the Vietnamese War in 1965 it was not certain that America would necessarily regard Vietnam as having priority over a Communist and anti-Communist civil war in Indonesia. As China could not in that case have rendered any effective assistance to the Communists in Indonesia, the consequences of an Indonesian Communist revolution might not have been assured, and the gains to China from any such development far from apparent.

It must be born in mind that China possessed no means of active military intervention in countries beyond the seas. Neither does she

now. Her ability, if she chooses, to move land armies of great numbers across her land frontiers is not in doubt. She did this in Korea.
If she has not done so in Vietnam it is because it was in any case
so far unnecessary, the Vietnamese needed weapons, not men, and
also because the essential cause for such intervention has not
materialized. This would be an American land invasion of North
Vietnam. The clearly understood fact that such an invasion would
involve Chinese intervention is probably the main reason why no
such invasion has taken place. But sea-borne military operations are
in a quite different category of possibilities. The Chinese navy is
small, and designed for coastal defence. The air force has no long
range bombers nor fighters, and is also designed for home defence.
China has not the shipping to move any large force across the sea.
All these reasons have prevented any Chinese attack upon the
dissident regime in Taiwan, the Nationalist held island. They
prevented the Chinese from securing the off-shore islands of Quemoy
and Matsu in 1958. They would completely rule out any expedition
which involved the despatch of troops to Indonesia or Malaysia—or
indeed any other overseas country. China could therefore give no
direct aid to Indonesian Communists, whether in power or not, if
American sea power was called in to frustrate any action by the
Indonesian Communists. It would have been hazardous and almost
prohibitively ineffective to try to send military supplies and arms to
Indonesian Communists whether forming the government of that
country or in revolt against it.

It is probable that the Peking policy makers had observed with
interest that when President Sukarno was faced with a revolt of the
military garrisons in the outer islands, and these had turned to
Nationalist China for support and supplies, even though such assistance was not opposed by any American sea power, it had been
singularly ineffective, and had failed to sustain the revolts. No
doubt there were other causes for this collapse, but the fact that
outside help from one of the Two Chinas had been invoked, and to
some degree supplied, but yet made no real difference, was significant.

Confrontation brought to notice the real weakness of any alliance
between China and Indonesia, which was that the only enemy which
they might have in common would be the Western powers, and that
these powers had complete command of the sea. Since China could
not sustain or even significantly help a Communist government or a
Communist revolt in Indonesia, the advantage to be gained from the
first was purely diplomatic. The Communist position in the world,
and the influence of Communist powers in Southeast Asia would be
enhanced. There was, even in this sphere, the doubtful aspect of the

Sino-Russian quarrel. The U.S.S.R. was the main supplier of armaments to President Sukarno, not China. It was to be expected that had his government come under Communist control this would still be the case. Indonesia as a Communist state might have moved into the Russian camp rather than into the Chinese one.

In September 1965 the underlying tensions between the Indonesian Communist Party and their opponents within the country burst out in the abortive coup of that month. The circumstances still remain very obscure, since only the accounts given by the side which triumphed, the army, have been given publicity. The thesis they propound is in the view of most observers much too simplified: that the Communist Party, aided by some dissident officers, attempted to take power and eliminate the principal army officers opposed to them; that they failed, and the people took a terrible vengeance upon the would-be rebels. There is, at least, no doubt about the last statement. Many tens of thousands, some estimates claim as many as half a million people, were massacred in all parts of Indonesia. Many of these were not full members of the Communist Party. Moreover, there is doubt whether the P.K.I. were in fact the originators of the coup, or merely sought to profit from a revolution which they had not directly instigated. Aidit, Secretary General of the P.K.I., was in Djakarta, but many of the leaders were not in Indonesia at that date. It seems at least strange that the leaders of a party planning a revolutionary coup apparently made such incredibly rudimentary preparations to back it up.

A second question is how far the Chinese were aware of what was going to happen, how far they were giving support to such a plan if the P.K.I. had one, and whether the kind of revolution which the Army claims to have crushed was in fact the kind which China had elsewhere encouraged and at times (as in Vietnam) had helped. Some of the Indonesian Communist Party leaders were in Peking, far from the scene of action. Had the Chinese been previously informed of the plot, it would seem very improbable that they would not have urged their Indonesian comrades to go home and take command. There is no evidence that the Peking authorities anticipated what was about to happen, nor had forewarning. They appeared to have been as much taken by surprise as all other observers, Communist and non-Communist alike. When the Indonesian leaders did return they were too late, their forces had not been mobilized nor prepared for revolution, they were overcome, and almost all the prominent members of the Party were tracked down, captured, and executed. This is certainly not the pattern of revolution which Mao Tse-tung had practised and preached.

On the other hand it does bear a striking resemblance to the course of events in China in 1927. Then the Communist revolutionary workers of Shanghai, organized and led by the Communist Party, seized the Chinese part of that city from the warlord who ruled it. A month or so later, when the main Nationalist army under Chiang Kai-shek arrived at Shanghai, after a few weeks of increasing tension between Army and Communist Party, Chiang Kai-shek carried out a sudden swift coup against the Communist Party, his nominal allies, in Shanghai; he arrested thousands of their followers, executed many hundreds, and only failed to catch their leaders (or some of them) by sheer chance. Later, when the Party was driven from power and hunted, two men, an obscure divisional general, Chu Teh, and a still minor figure, Mao Tse-tung, a rural revolutionary organizer, separately tried to raise a peasant and army revolt, and although at first very unsuccessful, gradually rebuilt the Party and its forces in the deep countryside of south China. Twenty-two years passed before the Chinese Communist Party was able to win full power.

This story, the saga of the Chinese Communist Party, through which its present leaders lived and fought, is to them, naturally, the real revolutionary experience. Soft roads to power had been betrayed and proved traps: only the hard road of insurrection, of guerrilla war, of rural bases and widespread peasant support, years of war and the continuing example to the people of a clean and efficient administration, can win power. The P.K.I. had not followed this road. They sought, like the Communist Party in China of 1925-27, to climb upon the backs of the army and the nationalist movement, to infiltrate, and to seize power at the right moment. It was the Russian, rather than the Chinese model for revolution. It seems probable that this in itself, by 1965, was not a point in favour of the P.K.I. in Chinese eyes. The failure of the type of revolutionary plot which had met with disaster in China forty years before would not surprise the Chinese; but it is also very improbable that they would have encouraged or expected such a movement to succeed. It is thus rather less than probable that Peking either knew of the intended coup (if the P.K.I. were really planning it) or would have given it encouragement had they known. To the Chinese Communists it was the wrong road to power, and moreover much too much on the Russian model.

It was, of course, nonetheless a serious set-back to Chinese policy. Their friends, mistaken or not, victims or failed conspirators, had been destroyed. The P.K.I. was decimated and continues under constant and ruthless suppression. Indonesia, reducing President Sukarno first to impotence and then deposing him, swung to the right, and has since then been ruled by the Army and its capable leader, President Suharto. Indonesia did not break off diplomatic relations with China, but these relations have been reduced to the minimum of aloof contact, and all aspects of co-operation between the two countries have vanished. The unfortunate resident Chinese, accused, in popular opinion, of complicity in the September plot, suffered further persecution, slaughter, and deprivation. Yet Indonesia did not move over to the camp of the Western Powers.

The policy of her rulers has been one of a kind of neutrality. Towards the Communist powers, the result of the September 1965 events has been to make relations cool or frigid, but not actively hostile. Towards the Western powers, the strength of Indonesian Nationalist feeling has precluded any overt association or dependence. Confrontation with Malaysia was first eased off then dropped. Indonesia remains in unchallenged possession of West Irian. Indonesia will put no bases at the disposition of the U.S.A. nor will she cease to purchase arms from Russia, if Russia is still willing to sell them on credit. The necessity which the Army still feels for maximizing the alleged danger of a Communist internal threat, in order to hold the people makes it difficult or impossible to re-establish friendly relations with China, and is even some impediment to relations with Russia. The former propaganda which portrayed Malaysia as the puppet of the British, and condemned the U.S.A. for intervention in Asia is well remembered and, one may suspect, approved by the people. But the operative factor preventing change in Indonesia's position is the traditional commitment to non-alignment.

For China, Indonesia has thus become a negative force; 'neither for us nor against us', no further help in establishing a Communist or Communist-aligned front in Southeast Asia, not likely to turn to revolution in the Communist manner for many years (but the hope, based on the corruption and economic weakness of the Army rule remains), and also no threat to China or to Chinese interests and policies. If China cannot, logistically, intervene in Indonesia (and her inability to do anything for the P.K.I. in its hour of need has conclusively demonstrated that') no more can Indonesia do anything in a positive way to harm China, even if such were the objectives of her rulers. But the evidence is rather that Indonesia would be willing to forget that China existed at all if it were possible. Present relations are therefore slight, and inactive. It does not seem that China has interested herself in the fate of the P.K.I. more than to give refuge to such of its leaders who were in China in September 1965, or who have arrived there since. The Party maintains an office in Peking, but this hospitality means very little in practice. It may be supposed that Chinese Communists are teaching their Indonesian guests what they believe to be the real programme for ultimate conquest of power. It is not at all evident that the programme is being implemented in Indonesia, nor that if it is in some small degree, China can render it any direct aid. Relations between the two countries are now slighter than they have been at any time since Indonesian independence and the victory of the Chinese Communist Party at home. What they may become in a changing East Asia is worth some speculative consideration.

Since the end of the close co-operation between the People's Republic of China and Indonesia following the September 1965 coup, many things have changed in Asia. The American Administration of President Nixon is committed, irrevocably, to a withdrawal from Vietnam and the 'Vietnamization' of the war in that country which is presented as a more credible alternative to the war-weary American people than it is likely to seem to be to Asians nearer the scene. Britain, in spite of the Conservative government's intention to maintain a 'presence' in the regions east of Suez, has manifestly mainly withdrawn from this region. Indonesia is rather more isolated than before. Her relations with China are cold; Russia is still far removed from actual on the spot power. The U.S.A., never involved in the Indonesian policies of the past except at second remove, is unlikely to now make any further or closer entanglement. These are the three which really matter, all others will play second fiddle to one or other of them.

Seen from the Indonesian point of view, relations with China are a problem. China will be there, right in the area, no matter what happens. The U.S.A. may withdraw further, or not so far, depending more on the vicissitudes of American politics than on the strategic realities of eastern Asia. In any case the whole region is really marginal to American interests and its former strategic importance much diminished or wholly destroyed by the development of inter-continental ballistic missiles, which would be the dominant weapon of any future world war now conceivable. America needs no South-east Asian bases to wage that type of war against either China or Russia, and before long China will equally be able to rely on her own territory to retaliate in kind upon the U.S.A. Thus Indonesia is unlikely to be wooed by either side so far as military considerations are concerned. China must be seen as unfriendly to a government which has massacred its Communist opponents, real and alleged,in such great numbers. Until, or unless, a government of a different complexion is established in Indonesia there is not much prospect of renewed co-operation and friendly relations.

Against this is the fact that China also has now only a slight, or at best an ideological interest in what happens to Indonesia. The Chinese, if faced with a world war in which they would not be the strongest contestant, would certainly not waste their strength on dangerous overseas expeditions of dubious value. They would con-centrate on home defence, and if sufficiently advanced in their nuclear programme, retaliation against the main antagonists. Indonesia would be outside this range of objectives. In the event of another world war continuing to be avoided, China's interest in Indonesia remains ideological. It would be good for China to have another large Communist partner in Southeast Asia. It could not be controlled by China (any more than Vietnam is controlled) but it would be a useful diplomatic ally. A revolution from the Left, or the coming to power of a government which was favourable, or not anti-Communist, would be equally satisfactory. A civil war following a Communist insurrection might not be so easy to handle. Ideologically China would be bound to give some support, however slight or mainly verbal, to the Communist side. This would provoke the ready suspicions of the Western world that more lay behind it. The result would be uncertain and the Chinese commitment too open for comfort.

Chinese policy does not necessarily require that all Southeast Asian nations should undergo Communist revolutions in every sort of circumstance. If things are otherwise favourable, this is no doubt the optimum outcome; but as matters will often be less simple and the risk of complications great, the type of change which installs a government not actively anti-Communist, willing to enter into friendly relations with China, and certain to deny bases to the U.S.A. is on the whole more desirable, at least as a first stage, which may last long. No reason for outside action or intervention is presented by this sort of development. The doctrine that every nation has the right to decide on its own form of government, if tattered, is still largely accepted. After the manifest failure to apply the contrary doctrine in Vietnam it is likely to gain wider support. It is therefore probable that China sees her best hope for future relations with Indonesia in these terms.

The prospect that the present or a future Indonesian government would go over wholly to the Western camp is not very real. National feeling, and the fact that Indonesia has really very little to offer for such an alliance are the obstacles. A country in grave economic difficulty is not likely to be a very welcome addition to the Western side in Southeast Asia; the cost could be very great. Equally, Indonesia does not now occupy the strategic situation which makes it of vital importance to the U.S.A. So long as the Suez Canal remains closed, the real lines of communication between the Pacific and the Atlantic Oceans are by way of the Cape of Good Hope. The prospect is therefore that between China and Indonesia there will be little change and not much visible rapprochement for many years to come.

Ultimately, this situation could not continue. The U.S.A. will cease to concern itself with the local affairs of Southeast Asia, which are really quite unimportant to her. Russia is far away, and if she contemplates a naval role in the Indian Ocean she has yet to acquire the bases on which this must rest. China is close, cannot be removed, and will grow more powerful within the next fifty years. Ultimately it is with China that Indonesia, like all other Southeast Asian countries, must deal. It is highly unlikely that China towards the end of the present century will have a government of very different complexion from its present one. Indonesia will have to treat with a Communist China, no matter whether the successors of Mao Tse-tung are his dedicated disciples or men who have somewhat differing ideas. In this relationship of the future the character and situation of the resident Chinese community in Indonesia is not likely to be a major factor. By that period the immigrant community will be absorbed, as second class citizens, or granted equal status with the long term descendants of early settlers. In either case they will have been divorced from direct contact with China for nearly half a century. Ethnically they may remain distinct, culturally they are certain to have become much more Indonesian—the prohibition of Chinese education being alone sufficient to achieve this result. Relations between the two countries will not turn on this question.

Trade, the increasing volume and power of Chinese industry and commerce will be a more important factor. For Indonesia it may be a necessity if her own economy is to make progress. Probably the most disregarded and yet the most significant fact about the next half century is that during this period China will have become a great industrial power, and the effects of this will be reflected not only, as at present, in a growing military capacity. For very long periods in the past trade was the only real contact between the two countries. It led to large scale Chinese immigration. This is not likely to be the consequence of future trading patterns, partly because on the Chinese side the trade will not be conducted by individual merchants, but by the state. It seems probable that the ancient relationship will prove the most enduring. Neither settlement by some few millions of Chinese in a far greater population of Indonesians could change the basic relationship, nor rather ephemeral political combinations, hostilities and alliances. The two countries, one tropical, the other temperate, have much to exchange between them; they developed this exchange of products at an early period, and it would seem certain that this relationship must prove the most long lasting.

Chapter Three

CHINA AND BURMA, THAILAND, AND THE PHILIPPINES

1. China and Burma

China and Burma, unlike most of the countries of Southeast Asia, have a long common frontier, between the Burmese Shan States and the Chinese province of Yünnan. On both sides the local inhabitants are neither Chinese nor Burmese, but members of a variety of minority peoples, some like the Shans, of higher culture, others such as the Wa, headhunters of a primitive tribal society. The frontier is more or less a modern concept which only assumed some reality after the British conquest of the old Burmese kingdom. Here, as in other parts of Asia, the older idea was that of a border zone rather than a defined and marked frontier. These zones were occupied by tribal groups, usually less developed than the ruling peoples in the neighbouring kingdoms or empires. Neither side actually administered the tribal region, authority ended with the last town or city inhabited by the dominant people. On the Burmese border this was Tengyueh on the Chinese side, Bhamo on the Burmese side. Between them was a wide region, taking five or six days to cross, which was under the local control of Shan princes or Kachin tribal chiefs.

Even in the days of the British Raj, before the Second World War, much of the old system remained. The actual frontier was unmarked and unguarded by police or military of either side. It was, indeed, rather difficult to know where it really was, and the maps used by China and by the British government in Burma showed wide discrepancies. Problems of the frontier peoples, raids, murders, banditry and other disputes used to be annually settled by a meeting of the British Commissioner for the Shan States and his Chinese opposite number, the senior official in charge at Tengyueh. Leisurely negotiations to define this frontier in more modern terms had proceeded for decades between Britain and the Chinese government, which for much of this period was not in real control of the province of Yünnan.

The frontier region is wild and jungle-covered, mountainous and crossed by great rivers. Its climate, warm, wet and in summer very hot, is unsuitable to the mountain people of Yünnan, which is a plateau lying on average at over five thousand feet and locally much higher. Chinese come down to trade and carry back the imported goods which find a market in Yünnan; they do not settle in these malarial lowlands. Thus nature had always defined the frontier rather better than the activities of rulers. It has not substantially changed since the Yünnan region first came under Chinese suzerainty in the third century A.D. In later times Yünnan, as the kingdom of Nanchao, was for more than six hundred years independent of and often very hostile to the Chinese empire. Ultimately it was the Mongols, not the Chinese, who conquered Nanchao and incorporated it in their Chinese empire. The Ming inherited this addition, the Manchus in turn took it over, and Yünnan became a Chinese province, even if it has continued to this day to be largely inhabited by minority peoples and retains many local peculiarities derived from its earlier non-Chinese culture. In the Nanchao period war with Burma was frequent, but the difficulties of communication and the difference of climate made any lasting occupation of Burmese territory impossible. Even the Mongols, who invaded and devastated Burma from Yünnan, ended by evacuating the country and leaving it to local turbulent feudatories. The frontier zone remained as it was, and still is, a region of small mixed tribes and principalities.

In this way the common frontier was not and need not be a very serious problem for China or for Burma. Trade passed across it, by mule caravan, and became a highly organized and locally important economic activity. China exported Ssuchuan silk by mule caravan for a distance of more than six hundred miles to Bhamo, whence it went by river steamer to Rangoon, and then on to Calcutta by sea. Burma sent back to China cotton thread, tobacco, jade, and a variety of light manufactured goods, but the caravans returning to China were usually only half laden, and the balance of trade favoured China. Not long before the Second World War the Chinese began to construct a motor road from Ssuchuan to Burma—the famous Burma Road—which was completed in the early stages of the Sino-Japanese War, and has been restored after the war to form a long and tenuous modern link between the two countries. Communications on the Burmese side were at the same time modernized to connect with the Chinese road.

The Chinese community resident in Burma does not, in large majority, derive from Yünnan, nor did it enter the country by the land route. The numbers, 320,000, are by comparison with other overseas Chinese communities in Southeast Asia rather small, and the vast majority reside in or near Rangoon, the capital, having come in by the sea route, from the same southeastern provinces of China which are the homelands of other overseas Chinese. Those who came from Yünnan are only a small community of innkeepers, caravan furnishers, mule dealers and similar occupations living by and servicing the caravan trade from Yünnan. They are virtually confined to Bhamo, the river port which is the terminal of the caravan route. Also, during the period of British rule in Burma, the Chinese immigrants did not have the dominating economic power which they acquired in other Southeast Asian countries. They had to compete with the Indians, who were much more numerous (500,000) and enjoyed the advantage of free access, being British subjects, and often had the further advantage of some knowledge of English. The Indian migrants came from south India, mainly being Hindu in religion, but with some Muslim money lenders among them. They tended to dominate the clerical employment in Burma, including the government service, and also played a prominent part in the professions, the retail trade, finance and local industry. These are the occupations which in other countries of the region had become almost Chinese monopolies, but in Burma the Chinese had no such hold on the national economy. Consequently they largely escaped the hostility which their situation elsewhere often arouses, and which in Burma was directed against the Indians. The Burmese, who had resented both the conquest (which, of the whole country, was late—1885) and the flood of Indian immigration it had brought, felt no kinship with India. They strongly resented, with some justification, being a mere province of the Indian empire, ruled by distant Delhi, and by men of Indian experience without direct knowledge of Burma. The Chinese are Buddhist, at least nominally, and in any case not fanatically attached to a religion which was alien to the Burmese. Burmese Buddhism, the Theravada system, had played a very prominent role in the life and social organization of the old kingdom. Buddhist Chinese did not offend Burmese susceptibilities in the way that Hindu or Muslim Indians ran the risk of doing.

Shortly before the Second World War, the British, recognizing that Burmese national resentment of the connection with India was real and in part at least justified, granted Burma dominion status, separate from India, with a considerable measure of self government. Whether this experiment, which was not wholly successful, would have resolved the problems of Burma in time is unknown, because the Japanese invasion in 1942 swept away British rule in any form. It also inflicted hardships upon the Chinese community, and led to a mass flight of Indians from the country. In the later stages of the war, north Burma became the theatre of war directed to reopening the road link with China, which except for a difficult air lift over the high mountain ranges, had been cut off from direct contact with her allies, the Western powers, since the Japanese conquest of Burma. Japan had allowed the Burmese nationalists to form a government and intended to grant Burma some sort of subservient independence after the war. The Burmese nationalists, realizing in 1945 that the Japanese were losing the war, changed sides, and brought their forces over to the allied cause. After the War it soon proved impossible to re-establish British rule in any form, and in January 1948 Burma was given full independence, choosing not to remain within the British Commonwealth.

Within a very few years of Burma's independence, the victory of the Chinese Communists in 1949 induced the governor of Yünnan, an old time military leader always rather independent of the Nationalist government in Nanking, to submit to the People's Republic, and the new regime was soon firmly established as sovereign in Yünnan. Some considerable force of Nationalist troops, commanded by a certain General Li Mi, then withdrew across the frontier into the Burmese Shan States, planning to continue resistance to the Communist regime from this secure base. It was secure, because the new Burmese government was not in control of the tribal and border zones; many of the tribes and minority peoples, such as the Karens, refused allegiance, being hostile to the Burmans, sometimes of a different religion (many Karens are Christian) and fearful of rule from Rangoon. The region of the border is in the climatic belt most favourable for the growing of the opium poppy, and the revenues from this illicit but very profitable and widespread trade were the sinews of Li Mi's resistance in the Shan States. The attitude of both Burma and China towards this situation was governed by diplomatic procedures. Burma had been among the first to recognize the People's Republic, and relations between the two governments were good. China naturally objected to the presence of armed forces in rebellion (as they saw it) against their government sheltering on the territory of a neighbour state. So did Burma; protests were made by Burma to the United Nations, but it was several years before the increasing scandal and the realization that the rebel army of Li Mi was receiving arms and supplies by secret air lift from Thailand and Nationalist held Taiwan—with American support—led to action which took out most of Li Mi's force by air to Taiwan and enabled the Burmese to recover at least partial control of the border zone. The remnants of Li Mi's force remain, living off the illicit opium trade, but keeping out of Chinese territory, and no longer affording any serious problem to the two countries.

Burma was itself subject to internal problems of great complexity. There were several dissident armies in the field; Communists of two factions, Karens, and other minorities. Control of the countryside was very slight for several years. The regime pursued a policy of 'Burmese Socialism' which was not far removed from a Communist economic policy, but could not be effectively implemented in the disturbed state of the country. Burma, in foreign affairs, was strictly non-aligned, and refused all accommodation for foreign military bases on her territory. This aspect of Burmese policy was very acceptable to the People's Republic of China. It is not apparent that China ever gave either of the two Communist dissident parties active support. It may be that their differences made any choice between them embarrassing and unrewarding; it is also important to recognize that Chinese Communist doctrine and practice is not to give open support to Communist rebellions unless these movements have established a government with which China can enter into diplomatic relations. Rebellion and revolution cannot be exported (whatever foreign critics may believe), they must be generated by the social forces within the country concerned. If these are strong enough to displace the previous regime, then they merit recognition as a new government expressing the will of the people; if they cannot attain this objective, they deserve sympathy as revolutionary fighters in the true cause, but not until they can win their own people to the true cause. In some ways this modern Chinese doctrine is reminiscent of the old Chinese doctrine of the 'Mandate of Heaven' (T'ien Ming). The leader, who begins as a rebel, but ends as the emperor, has achieved the Mandate of Heaven—divine approval of his struggle. He henceforth is 'legitimate'; the fallen house is no longer legitimate and its claims inadmissable. In other words, success is always right, failure is condemned. The rebel who fails receives no accolade from Heaven. The People, as in other Chinese Communist doctrines, have taken the place of Heaven.

From this point of view it was always clear enough that the government of Burma in Rangoon, under successive leaders, was in fact the only effective government in the country. Gradually the rebels were losing ground. China was therefore willing to enter into further negotiations for the definition of the frontier between the two countries which still remained very largely indeterminate. These negotiations were pursued, amicably it would appear, for some years, and in 1960 yielded an agreement, which to the surprise of many critics of the Chinese regime, gave Burma title to large tracts which China had claimed in British days. It is true that much of this area, along the course of the Salween river in northeastern Burma, had never been under British administration, and some places in it had actually for years been the seat of local Chinese magistrates, although shown on British maps as within Burma. Cartographical imperialism was a feature of the late nineteenth century not confined to Burma. The frontier in the wild Wa headhunters region was also defined with some concessions to Burmese claims; perhaps here the Chinese felt no burning ardour to acquire jurisdiction over and responsibility for these difficult citizens. The Sino-Burmese Border delimitation agreement, conducted in respect of wild and difficult country very little known and inaccurately mapped, yet brought to an amicable solution largely in favour of the weaker party, stands in marked contrast to the failure of the Sino-Indian negotiations to reach any solution of the problems of the Tibetan-Indian border, which in most respects are very similar indeed to those of the border between Yünnan and Burma. In Tibet, the country is higher, harsher, less inhabited and economically even less valuable than the Burmese border jungles. In the eastern section above Assam, the tribes are equally neither Indian nor Chinese, rather backward and economically retarded. But the government of India has consistently refused to admit any possibility of negotiation, taking the stand that these ill-defined borders are in fact precise frontiers established by the British Raj. The Chinese do not accept this interpretation, and have good evidence for their view; they have offered to settle by negotiation, but India has never agreed, and the contest broke into open fighting in 1962 when India endeavoured to enforce its claims.

The successful settlement of the frontier problem between China and Burma marked the high point of Sino-Burmese relations since the independence of Burma and the accession to power of the Chinese Communist Party. There does not seem at any time to have been any overt trend in China to reassert the ancient relationship of suzerain and tributary which prevailed until the British conquest of Burma. It is true that it was for many years more formal than real. The last intervention of China in Burma was in the mid-seventeenth century, when the last Ming Pretender, having been driven from Yünnan to Burma, where he received support from the king, was pursued by the Chinese army in the service of the new Manchu dynasty. Here the Chinese defeated the Burmese forces, and compelled the king to surrender the last Ming for execution. Under the Ch'ing (Manchu) dynasty Burma continued to send a triennial tribute mission to Peking. An elephant, which had to accomplish the long march of about two thousand miles from the border to Peking, was a principal element in this tribute. The duty of equipping this mission had been farmed out upon a family of

Burmese nobility, who continued to carry it out, by routine, even after the British conquest, until this anomaly was brought to the attention of Calcutta.

The Cultural Revolution in China in 1966 and subsequent years brought about a sharp change in the tone of Sino-Burmese relations. Enthusiasm for the new doctrine, the Thought of Mao Tse-tung, infected the young resident Chinese in Rangoon, and many began to wear Mao buttons on their coats, to demonstrate, and to extol their leader, and in other ways to manifest a national chauvinism mixed with revolutionary zeal which had not been at all conspicuous in the Chinese community hitherto. The Burmese resented these attitudes. They are a people of strong national identity, rather suspicious of foreigners, and although individually charming and courteous, tend as a nation to be aloof and often seek to withdraw from close contact with foreign peoples. Perhaps their history of frequent large scale intrusion of foreign powers, Chinese, Thai, Mongol, Indian, British, has bred this outlook; it has characterized the regime of General Ne Win who displaced the civilian regime of U Nu formerly in power (1962). In a political climate in which foreign presence is as far as possible excluded, and the country is largely closed to alien visitors, the Chinese exuberance in favour of the Cultural Revolution aroused antagonism and fear. Riots against the Chinese broke out in Rangoon, and there was some loss of life. The Burmese government blamed the Maoist enthusiasts, the Chinese government, then under the strong pressure of Red Guard extremism, retaliated by denouncing the government of Burma in very harsh terms. Relations deteriorated rapidly. The Chinese ambassador was withdrawn. It is true that so were all other ambassadors from posts in all parts of the world except Cairo, and too much significance cannot be placed upon this feature in respect of Burma alone. But it served to increase suspicion that the China of the post-Cultural Revolution might become a more dangerous neighbour than the government which had concluded the border agreement and taken an understanding attitude to the problem of Li Mi and his forces.

Since the Cultural Revolution officially came to a successful conclusion in April 1969, and the control of the Chinese Foreign Office was recovered from Red Guard occupation, there has been in respect of Burma, as elsewhere, a slow and cautious return to more normal relations. The only real problem between the two countries is the fact, made evident by the troubles in 1966 and 1967, that in spite of the careful policy of restraint practised before the Cultural Revolution, and known to have been endorsed by Chou En-lai himself when he was in Burma in 1956, many local and in particular

young Chinese in Burma have remained very conscious of their
ethnic affinity and under strong cultural influence from the ancestral
home country. The Chinese in Burma are not one of the largest of
the overseas communities, but they are cohesive, live mainly in one
great city, the capital, and have since the departure of most of the
Indian population the conspicuous character of a large alien population, prosperous, economically strong, and apparently still imbued
with feelings of national identity to their original homeland. These
are aspects which Burmese are not willing to accept with goodwill.
Until the character of Chinese policy in the post-Cultural Revolution
era in respect of the overseas Chinese is clearer than is yet the case,
it is not possible to foresee how this problem will be approached.

2. China and Thailand

Although separated only by a relatively narrow strip of Burmese and
Laotian territory, and thus appearing almost contiguous on a map,
China and Thailand are not in effective close contact physically.
The zones in between them have no, or very bad communications,
and on both sides the national territory is sparsely inhabited, often
by minority peoples. The intermediate area has never been an
avenue of free passage between China and the Chao Phraya valley,
the heart of Thailand. No recorded example of a Chinese invasion of
Thailand by this route exists. In effect the large numbers of Chinese
who settled in Thailand from the late eighteenth century onward
came by sea, and the majority are from the same southeastern
provinces, in this case north Kuangtung, from which the other
overseas communities derived. In earlier historical times contact
between China and Thailand was slight, although of long standing.
The trade route round the coast of Vietnam would seem to be very
old, and the degree of assimilated Chinese in the Thai ethnic composition suggests a long connection, if not necessarily one based on
very large numbers. Thailand was a rather nominal tributary in
the Ming and Manchu periods but this status lapsed without protest
or conflict when in the nineteenth century the power of China was
manifestly on the wane. During this period much larger numbers of
Chinese migrated to Thailand, drawn by the developing economy
and the facility of sea passages in European ships. The pattern of
immigration was very'similar to that which prevailed in the countries
which were under European colonial rule.

Once arrived, however, the Chinese migrant did find a rather
different environment from that offered by Malaysia or Indonesia
under the British and the Dutch. In this period there was no

limitation on what a Chinese might do to gain a living, including the service of the king. Many rose high in that service, often being granted titles and honours, and not infrequently taking Thai names and becoming at least partially assimilated. The number of 'Thais' who are of part Chinese descent is unquestionably large, but it is not recorded in modern census taking, nor in earlier archives. Thailand is not now and was not a hundred years ago an overpopulated country. There is room for all, and the Chinese who migrated there were not thought to be taking the bread from the mouths of others, nor occupying land which rightly belonged to natives. For the most part the Chinese lived in the cities, above all in the capital, Bangkok; and engaged in urban pursuits, shopkeeping, rice milling, banking, and the professions. They became an indispensable part of the economy, but for many years this situation did not seem to trouble the minds of the kings of Thailand. Chinese women, up to the fall of the empire, came only in small numbers; Chinese therefore inter-married with Thai, and this helped assimilation, even if the children were usually classed as Chinese.

The overthrow of the Manchu Dynasty and the concurrent change in opinion, not only in Thailand, about the role of the Chinese migrant, caused the beginning of a new, less smooth relationship. With the fall of the dynasty the overseas Chinese who had contributed handsomely to the funds of the revolutionary party gained a new status in their homeland. They were now honoured citizens living abroad, rather than outcasts, near criminal fugitives, as the Manchu dynasty had tended to treat them. Women came freely to join their relatives and to marry young men among the migrant population. The Chinese community not only grew rapidly but assumed a much more distinctively Chinese character. This was helped by the rapid spread of education among the Chinese, and the character of that education which was based on current models and textbooks of Republican China. These had a strong nationalist content. Young Chinese not only now learned to read, but were also imbued with national consciousness. The community began to seem more alien, and less assimilated than it had been. It was inevitable that this development aroused the nascent nationalism of the Thais themselves. In the early decades of the twentieth century the European characteristic disease, or peculiarity, modern national-ism, spread to Asia. Hitherto, in most parts of that region a man's religion rather than his race or allegiance had been seen as significant. A Muslim felt alienated from a Hindu or a Buddhist even if they spoke the same language and were ethnically closely akin. Chinese assimilated easily in Buddhist countries such as Burma and Thailand, but not in Muslim countries such as Malaysia or Indonesia.

This outlook, under the influence of the Western education which the leaders of the younger generation now received in Europe, began to change. The weakness of Asian states, the subservient status of colonies, which once had been proud kingdoms, was attributed to the lack of national consciousness of their peoples. The idea that the spread of migration portended ultimate military invasion and conquest by the home country of migrants began to be entertained, and was indeed promoted by leading nationalist thinkers, including no less a person than King Rama VI of Thailand (1910-1925). The logical possibility cannot, of course be denied. If an alien race does become a majority in a new country into which it has migrated, it may well end by becoming politically dominant and ultimately regard the land as its own. Examples such as the European movement into North America, or into Australia, illustrate the extreme case. But these countries had only very light and relatively backward native populations. The situation in Southeast Asia was not strictly comparable. The Chinese tended to assimilate in Thailand rather than to become an exclusive foreign group; if this latter trend began to increase in the late nineteenth and still more in the early twentieth century it was largely due to passing factors. Twenty years later the pattern of assimilation was still very evident in social life in Thailand.

This view was not taken by the nationalist politicians, mostly of military origin, who came to power in 1932 when the absolute monarchy was shorn of direct executive power. They soon developed a system of discriminatory legislation against the Chinese residents, which has persisted until the present time, although often rendered rather ineffective by the real dependence of the economy on the Chinese and the willingness of all concerned to turn a blind eye on many obvious evasions. But fearing the influence of Chinese consuls and an embassy in the days of Nationalist control, the government in Bangkok steadfastly refused to enter into diplomatic relations with the Republic of China. This was the situation up to the Second World War. Thailand was then compelled to join the Japanese alliance, but evaded the worst consequences of being on the defeated side by a prompt and timely unconditional surrender. However, the kingdom was compelled to open diplomatic relations with China, which had been on the winning side. Discrimination against the Chinese was continued, and the Nationalist government, already facing the challenge of the Communists in a new civil war, was unable to make any effective protest. When the Nationalist government fell in 1949, Thailand broke off relations with China and has not recognized the People's Republic.

Anti-Communism was given as the reason for this attitude, but it really masks the far older attitude which was simply anti-Chinese.

Pridi Panomyang who had been the first post-war Prime Minister, was displaced in 1947 by Pibul Songramm who had been a collabora- tor with the Japanese. Pridi then took refuge in Peking and this emphasized the hostility between the two governments. The Chinese community has undoubtedly suffered more suspicion and discrimina- tion as a result, but the government in Peking has had no means of relieving their plight. In any case it is not among the resident Chinese that the subversionary tactics of the Communists, inside or outside the country, are seen to have effect, but among the depressed rural population of the northeast of Thailand, a poor region, and among the Malay population of the extreme south, bordering upon Malaysia, where national and still more religious motivation is operative. This anti-Chinese stance of the Thai government is sometimes controlled by prudence. When Malaysia lifted the embargo on the export of rubber to China, Thailand, much more vociferously anti-Communist, hastened to do the same, lest she should lose a valuable market.

Thailand is a traditional enemy of Cambodia; and Cambodia, under Sihanouk, was a neutral favoured by Peking. This alignment did nothing to improve relations between China and Thailand, and the involvement of Thai troops in the Vietnamese war on the side of Saigon marked the contrast of attitudes to a quarrel which did not directly concern either country. Thailand was also a base for U.S. heavy bomber flights to bomb the Ho Chi Minh trail in Laos and North Vietnam. In Chinese eyes the Thais were thus engaged in the war, and the retaliation which they have adopted, of arming and assisting with supplies the Thai insurgents in the northeast of the country, no doubt appears a logical and legitimate riposte to American use of Thai bases. It would appear that the Thais are now beginning to reassess the situation to which their previous policies have led them. America is not going to maintain a large military presence in Southeast Asia, but China is there by the facts of geography. There has been some indication that with the changing American attitude to China and the widespread movement among other nations towards recognition of Peking and the establishment of normal relations, the rulers of Thailand have become aware that they might be left in dangerous isolation.

As elsewhere, the only real problem between Thailand and China is the situation and future of the Chinese community. There is no common frontier, and no threat of land invasion. The insurgency in northeast Thailand does not, at least so far, appear to present a real risk of revolution, but rather emphasises the need for reforms and development in a neglected region. It is probably supported by China as an anti-American move connected with the U.S. bases in the same region. Should this form of U.S. participation in the war diminish or cease, it would seem probable that Chinese activity among the insurgents would also fall away. The doctrine that revolution cannot be exported to countries which have not produced their own revolutionary situations could certainly apply to Thailand. It may be some time before normal relations between China and Thailand emerge; but the changes in major policies now taking place in East Asia could indicate much more rapid progress than was to be expected only a short time ago. Thailand has a national tradition of rapid and skilful adjustment to the threat of outside superior force; the kingdom was saved from extinction in the nineteenth century by the brilliant exercise of this type of policy by the Kings Mongkut and Chulalangkorn. At the end of the Second World War a similar *volte face* was performed. The need to adopt such a policy may not yet be pressing, but it cannot be denied that Thai tradition provides the models for such a transformation should it become the best solution to a dangerous situation.

3. China and the Philippine Republic

The Philippine archipelago is the nearest of all the overseas Southeast Asian countries to China; and the historical contact, although not so old as that with the continental countries, runs back nearly one thousand years. Archaeological finds have shown that some trade existed in the T'ang period (seventh to ninth centuries A.D.) and some early records of foreign lands beyond the seas, which some scholars hopefully interpreted as proof of a Chinese discovery of America, have been shown to be more consistent, and probable, as evidence of Chinese contact with the Philippines. The islands, before the intrusion of Malay rulers into the most southerly, and the subsequent conquest of the main group by the Spaniards in the sixteenth century, had not evolved a higher culture able to leave local records. Politically they were fragmented between many tribes. When the Ming imperial fleets visited the islands in the early fifteenth century, it would have been very easy to impose Chinese rule and settle the country with Chinese immigrants. Some such limited programme, the establishment of permanent bases for the fleet, seems to have been suggested. But the overriding decision to abandon all naval activity and power eliminated this possibility. A century later the Spaniards had taken the country.

Under the rule of Spain the Philippines were developed on feudal lines, but there was an acute shortage of skilled manpower. The native Filipinos were not acquainted with the technology of building, metal working and many other necessary crafts. Chinese immigrants came in large numbers to supply this need. They also undertook retail trade and a variety of occupations which the Spanish land-owning and official class—virtually the totality of the Spanish population—were unwilling to enter. Numbers grew rapidly, and the Spaniards became suspicious of the potential strength of the migrant Chinese. Also they did not readily convert to the Catholic religion, obstinacy which in the eyes of the Spanish rulers of that age was certainly a sin, and very nearly a crime. There were two major massacres of the Chinese population (in 1603 and 1639) followed by expulsion of the survivors and prohibition of immigration. But policy had soon to be reversed as, when the Chinese were gone, the economy of the country collapsed. A third massacre (1662) was only averted by the intercession of the Archbishop of Manila, and a third expulsion only reversed when the obscurantist government in Madrid was, with difficulty, brought to understand that this measure would ruin the country. Thereafter the Chinese were allowed to survive, and to grow rich.

The U.S.A., having defeated Spain in the Spanish-American War of 1898, took over the government of the Philippines under a system which repudiated the colonial status, but while preparing the islands for self government it had to operate in practice much as any other colonial regime. In 1903 a census was taken which gave the figures for the Chinese population as 41,000, but it is generally conceded that this number is too low, since many thousands concealed their ethnic identity, for fear that the census was a preliminary to dis-crimination or expulsion. There is no evidence at all that any such intention was held by the American administration, but a long tradition of persecution by the Spaniards had left a deep suspicion of any government policy. It can hardly be said to have been wholly unjustified, for since attaining complete independence the Philippine government has adopted a wide range of discriminatory practices and laws directed against the Chinese community. In the period before the war the then government of China maintained consular posts in the Philippines, which was not yet a sovereign independent state. After the war, the achievement of full independence coincided very closely, as elsewhere in Southeast Asia, with the coming to power of the Chinese Communists. The Philippine Republic, still closely guided in its international relations by the U.S.A., refused to recognize the People's Republic of China, and has never done so.

There have therefore been no diplomatic relations between China and the Philippines, and trade was also under a strict embargo. Immigration from the mainland ceased. Relations with the National-ist regime on Taiwan (an island not very distant from the northern

Philippines) have remained aloof and cool; the rulers of the Philippine Republic, like those of Thailand, are basically motivated by anti-Chinese sentiments, and whether the Chinese be Red or White has only marginal importance to them. The fact that mainland China was under the Communist regime was an excellent cover for discrimination against the Philippine Chinese. Protected against the possible consequences of these policies by the geographical situation of the islands and the power of the American navy, the Philippine regimes of successive presidents have at no time modified their anti-Chinese policy, nor sought any accommodation with Peking. It is interesting to observe that many of the most vociferously anti-Chinese politicians have all the appearance of being largely of Chinese origin in their ethnic stock. This phenomenon, also conspicuous in Thailand, is not unusual in many other parts of the world. Extreme nationalists are quite often in part descended from the peoples whom they regard as hereditary enemies.

Chapter Four

CHINA AND MALAYSIA AND SINGAPORE

The surrender of Japan and the conclusion of the Pacific War in September 1945 produced profound changes in Southeast Asia, and not least in the fortunes of the overseas Chinese communities established in greater or lesser strength in all these countries. But the changes were not exactly what the victors expected or desired. On the one hand the overwhelming power of Japan in the region disappeared, but was replaced by the much greater power of the U.S.A. The colonial powers who had hoped to recover their lost empires found that the American people and the administration of President Truman had only, at best, a tepid enthusiasm for any such restoration. Colonialism was an unpopular term in the U.S.A., and in spite of the facts of U.S. rule in such places as Samoa and Guam, and her over-riding suzerainty in pre-war Philippines, Americans would repudiate the suggestion that they too were colonialists. As has been seen in previous chapters, this U.S. attitude led to the early termination of Dutch attempts to recover Indonesia from the nationaalist republicans of that country, and in Vietnam the U.S. only supported the French when it became clear that the nationalist, anti-colonial revolt was led by the Communist Vietminh. Even then the Americans soon preferred to give whole hearted aid to anti-Communist regimes in South Vietnam rather than intervene on behalf of the failing colonial power. Britain recovered her authority in Malaya, Burma and Borneo by her own efforts, and in the case of Hong Kong only by an independent initiative taken without consultation or agreement with the supreme U.S. command in the Western Pacific.

Paradoxically the people in Southeast Asia who were most ready to welcome the return of the British were the Chinese overseas communities, for they alone had endured the full harshness and hostility of the Japanese occupiers, and they alone had produced no collaborators with the enemy. It may not be true that they welcomed their status as quasi-aliens in a colonial empire, but they had found it preferable to that of the most oppressed minority under Japanese rule. Their continued support for the allied cause, through its darkest hours, the fact that they had maintained a small but not ineffective guerrilla resistance in Malaya, and had aided British and allied prisoners and fugitives, all led many to expect that when British authority was restored their status would be reviewed and improved. China under the Kuomintang government of Chiang Kai-shek was an ally of Great Britain; so the Chinese, whether British citizens or immigrants, were surely friends.

As in Indonesia, where to be known as the friends of the Dutch was to prove a disastrous liability, so in Malaya the Chinese expectations encountered the opposition of the Malays. The first proposed reorganization of the country, in 1946, the Malayan Union, which would have improved the national status of the Chinese immigrants, and diminished the authority of the Malay sultans, led to the rise of a Malay nationalist party (United Malays National Organisation) which demanded a different reform, one which took account of their claim to be the natives of the land and entitled to a politically privileged position to offset the economic dominance of the Chinese community. British policy yielded to this demand: the constitution was revised, and Singapore excluded from the new Malayan Federation (1948). This led to strong Chinese protest. The exclusion of Singapore, the most advanced community in the country, from political rights conferred on the sultanates seemed to many Chinese a most unfair and prejudiced decision. It was attributed, not without reason, to the Malay-minded majority of the British colonial service senior officers.

These early years after the surrender of Japan were marked by another development, which was in part at least, prejudicial to the Chinese community. The guerrillas who had fought the Japanese in the jungle were, in the vast majority, of Chinese race. At the surrender they had been honoured and decorated. But they were also Communists. They did not willingly nor fully accept disbandment and the handing in of their arms. Much was concealed in jungle hideouts. The Communist Party soon turned to industrial action with a strong political purpose. Government reaction was resisted and resented; before long the Communist Party declared open insurrection and took to the jungles once more (1948). The Malayan Emergency had begun. This campaign of terrorism and guerrilla fighting was to last for several years, and at first to reduce much of the country to a state of great insecurity. The Party membership was at least 90 per cent Chinese, and this fact cast a certain suspicion upon all of the Chinese community, even though, in fact, more victims of the terrorist campaign were of Chinese stock than of any other community.

At the same time that the situation in Malaya was taking a turn unfavourable to the expectations and aspirations of the Chinese community, a change in China itself both enhanced these local difficulties and brought a wholly new factor into play. At the end of 1949 the Kuomintang government, for two years losing the last civil war, was finally driven from the mainland to the island refuge of Taiwan; and the People's Republic of China, the Communist regime, was proclaimed in Peking on 1 October 1949. The homeland of the immigrant Chinese was now under a Communist government, in a position, should it choose to do so, to put any type of pressure upon the families and relations of a very large part of the overseas Chinese community. Many things were now to be changed; hitherto the Chinese community had looked to China as the homeland, respectable in the eyes of colonial rulers as an ally in the recent war. The overseas Chinese had contributed funds for defence and reconstruction, even if many were disillusioned by what they had learned of the misuse of these funds. The complexities of the situation were hardly simplified by the British decision to recognize the new Chinese government, made early in January 1950. On the one hand Britain, as the colonial power, was waging a difficult war against a Communist insurrection in Malaya, in which the insurgents were mainly recruited from the Chinese community; on the other, they had recognized an avowedly Communist government as the legal government of China itself.

The great majority of the Chinese in Malaya were not Communists, nor inclined to that Party; but they were strongly Chinese in national sentiment, way of life, language and culture. China under the new regime soon showed that it was once more united after a dreary fifty years of disunion and confusion, that it was embarked on a vast plan of industralization and modernization, long overdue, but certain to bring about a major industrial revolution in the most numerous people on the earth, the kith and kin of the overseas Chinese themselves. China was also, in 1950, only one year later, to prove in Korea that she was able to beat back an American army and defend her ally, North Korea, from imminent conquest. These dramatic changes could not fail to impress the overseas Chinese and create a totally new image of their ancestral land. For nearly half a century, if not more, the overseas Chinese, stimulated by the patriotism which often grows faster in detached communities than in the home environment, had hoped for the rejuvenation of China, and contributed hard earned money to any cause which seemed to promise that result. Now they had got it; but it was brought about by a Communist regime which their colonial rulers were manifestly both afraid of and opposed to. Yet the government in Britain itself had recognized this new Communist regime, and continued in relations with it even when British troops serving in the United Nations forces in Korea were fighting Chinese volunteers who had intervened on behalf of hard pressed North Korea. These thin disguises may have satisfied the sophisticated procedures of high policy and diplomacy, but they were not so easily understood by the ordinary citizen.

Nor were these the only paradoxes. China had been recognized by Britain, therefore all Chinese Consulates in Malaya, of which there were several in most of the large cities where Chinese were numerous, became the property of the Peking regime, and they had the treaty right to appoint new staff to these posts. Such officers would certainly be Communists, or at least trusted servants of a Communist regime. Yet all around these cities a deadly guerrilla war was raging carried on by Malayan Communists of Chinese race. Not unnaturally the British officials saw the prospect with great dismay. In every major city there would be a diplomatically protected haven and headquarters for the insurgents. In Singapore itself, the premises of the Bank of China, now under Communist Peking's control, displayed for all to see a large inscription in the handwriting of Chairman Mao Tse-tung himself. At this time the works of all Communist writers from Marx to Mao were prohibited literature in Malaya and Singapore.

The British also had the treaty right to open up their Consulates in China, of which there had been a large number before the war, many still occupied. But strangely, the new Chinese government made no appointments to the Consulate posts in Malaya, and soon showed a great unwillingness to permit the continuance or reopening of all but a minimum number of British Consulates in China. In fact the Peking government never appointed any consular staff in Malaya, and in the course of a few years the British Consulates in China were reduced to Shanghai alone, and that terminated in 1966.

This strange abstention on the part of the Peking government, so confidently accused of plans of large scale subversion throughout Southeast Asia, remains an enigma. It may be explained by a closer look at what the policy of Peking towards the overseas Chinese communities of the Nanyang was to become. The evidence that this policy was not at all what most foreign opinion believed it to be is conclusive, since the Cultural Revolution has revealed much that was long hidden. At the time, the early years of the regime in

Peking, contemporary with the Emergency in Malaya, it was observed that Peking's propaganda and news of the insurrection always scrupulously referred to the 'Malayan Communist Party' and never by hint or word revealed to its readers that this party was in fact overwhelmingly Chinese in recruitment. When the British authorities, in order to deprive the insurgents of supplies, removed the large settlements of rural Chinese squatter farmers, who had fled to the country from Japanese oppression in the cities, and resettled these people in new villages under police or military protection, the Peking Press contained long and heart-rending accounts of the sufferings of these oppressed and innocent peasants. But there was never a word to reveal that they were Chinese. They were 'Malayans'.

It is readily accepted today that the policies of Communist regimes are to be assessed better by what is not said than by what is made explicit. The careful avoidance of the word 'Chinese' in all publicity concerning the Malayan Emergency is therefore an important indication. It means that Peking did not wish her own people, to whom this publicity is primarily directed, to realize that the Malayan insurrection was a Chinese manned movement, nor that the Chinese communities such as the squatter farmers who were caught up in the guerrilla war were also of Chinese race. Had this been made clear, it would be difficult to explain why China herself had not rushed to the defence and liberation of her oppressed fellow countrymen. Communist movements everywhere have the sympathy of Communist governments; the world expects this, and accepts it, more or less with resignation. But sympathy is one thing, aid and active support is another. China could not aid the Malayan insurgents, Communist and Chinese though they were, without a head-on conflict with Great Britain, which could only have been either frustrating or involved a still wider conflict. China had no naval forces and her air force was designed for short range, defensive operations. Malaysia is at least a thousand miles by sea from the nearest point on China's south coast, and that sea was dominated by American, and to some degree by British naval power. Intervention was impossible.

The new Chinese government was at this time, as subsequently, continuing a campaign of opposition to 'imperialism' and declaring to its citizens that the Revolution was a great victory over imperialism, which was a defeated and declining force, destined to utter destruction. In Korea the actual strength of the Chinese army could be deployed across a common frontier to drive back the advance of General MacArthur and his American army. This could be, and was, hailed as a great victory in China, and treated as such by many overseas Chinese not themselves Communists. But no such victory could be attained in distant Malaya; it would not be at all satisfactory for this fact to be inconveniently obvious, as would have happened had China openly intervened or openly supported the Malayan insurgents. There was good reason for obscurity in the language of the publicity media, and for refraining from opening Consulates which would have raised hopes that could not be fulfilled, and made difficulties which China could not adequately overcome.

Meanwhile another political change also made a policy of caution more desirable. It became clear that the best and perhaps the only hope of suppressing the Communist insurrection in Malaya was to speed up the grant of independence to the whole country, and thus remove one most important source of support for the insurgents, their claim to be fighting 'colonial imperialism' for the liberation of the country. When the British returned to Malaya in 1945 it is not at all clear, or perhaps probable, that they contemplated giving the country its independence for many years. The question was not believed to be at all urgent. The Malays had shown very little nationalist sentiment before the war, the Chinese had seemed content with their economic predominance even if this meant political exclusion. But events in Burma, where British rule was barely restored before it was found necessary to hand over to Burmese nationalism if a bloody and prolonged conflict was to be avoided, the progress of India towards independence, and the general realization that the colonial empires had outlived their time, altered all these preconceptions. The winds of change were not yet blowing in Africa, but they had attained gale force in Asia.

All that was needed was that there should be some strong evidence that Malays and Chinese would not make the morrow of independence the first day of a communal struggle in which the country would succumb to chaos. The leaders of the two communities had the wisdom to realize that compromise would win all, and intransigence could only be frustrating. An alliance of the leading Malay Party (U.M.N.O.) and the Malayan Chinese Association assured that elections would be contested by a nascent coalition, and that splinter and left-wing groups would not gain any serious ascendancy. This was what the British wanted—a way out, with dignity, decency and a solid assurance that their departure would not mean leaving the country to chaos. They got it, and they went (1957).

It is not possible to know exactly how the Chinese government in Peking evaluated this development. Their open attitude was to cast doubt and disbelief on any move made by the 'imperialist powers' however liberal, as a trick, a deceitful action designed to secure the essential advantages of capitalist imperialism while giving away some outworn trappings of colonial pomp. It is of course true that British investments in Malaya were not jeopardized by independence, and might have suffered far more from a prolonged guerrilla war. Never-theless Peking must have known that what had now happened was an event of crucial significance. Henceforward Malaya would be ruled by a coalition of Malays and Chinese, in which the Malays held the predominant political position, modified by the continuing economic prominence of their Chinese colleagues. The insurrection was deprived of its main appeal, and indeed soon dwindled down to a hard core hiding out on the Thailand frontier of Malaya.

The attitudes of the Chinese towards China itself remained some-what ambivalent. The wealthy classes, certainly not inclined to Communism, were nonetheless confronted with more idealistic youths, often of their own families, who were more impressed by the might and growth of the new China than disturbed by its economic and social policies. A curious example of this attitude of mind was the generally accepted view that no institution, educational or non-political though it might be, and however hard pressed for funds, could possibly accept the ample assistance which the American Foundations would have been ready to provide. This opinion was held both by very senior British officials, by Chinese educators, and by Chinese millionaires. America had opposed, and under the guid-ance of John Foster Dulles, Secretary of State, continued to oppose and to denounce the People's Republic. This was simply not accep-table to most overseas Chinese, no matter what their own political views might be. The affairs of China, they felt, were for China to settle; the presumption, all too familiar from the days of colonial and imperialist pressure, that the Western world could or should dictate to China her form of government or her national policy was no longer to be tolerated.

There was also the consideration that although the Peking govern-ment was not an enthusiastic friend to the newly independent Malaya, it was also now obvious to those who studied the facts, that Peking was not an active or effective supporter of the defeated insurgents of the Emergency. Peking, in effect, had also to adjust to the new world of nation states in Southeast Asia, and it is important to realize how close in time the coming to power of the Communist Party in China was to the attainment of independence in most of Southeast Asia. The Peking People's Republic was proclaimed on 1 October 1949, and full control of all Chinese territory other than Taiwan was achieved by the end of that year. Indonesia won full independence from Holland in the same year. Burma had been given her indepen-dence in January 1948 and India and Pakistan had achieved the same goal in 1947; Malaya not until 1957. The former British colonies in north Borneo, Sarawak and Sabah, did not gain complete independence before becoming part of the new Malaysian federation in 1963. Thus between the establishment of the People's Republic in October 1949, and the independence of Malaya in 1957, the last of the major colonies to attain this status, only eight years had passed, and for most of the former dominions and colonies independence was gained even before the Chinese Communist Party had come to full power.

There are certain strange contrasts between China's relations with the countries considered in the last chapter, Burma, Thailand and the Philippines, and her relations with Malaysia and the island city state of Singapore. China has relations with Burma, although not with Thailand and the Philippine Republic; nor does she have diplomatic relations with either Malaysia or Singapore. But in other respects there are unexpected divergences in the relationship. In Burma, Thailand and the Philippines, as also in Indonesia, the Chinese community, although often large in actual numbers, is but a small proportion of the whole population. Yet it is in these countries (Burma excepted) that there is the most harsh discrimination against the Chinese, although in these countries they have no political power as a community, and no expectation of equal or overriding political authority. In Malaysia and in Singapore, on the other hand, the Chinese are either a very large proportion of the total population or, as in Singapore, the strong majority. They already have considerable political power, and the possibility that they will or might dominate these countries is certainly not unreal. Yet in these lands where the possibility of Chinese predominance is not to be discounted, there is very little discrimination against the Chinese community: none in economic matters, and only in Malaysia is there some reservation of civil service posts and also a dominant political power reserved to the Malays. So whereas the Chinese in Thailand, Indonesia and the Philippines are unquestionably under some oppression, the Chinese of Malaysia and Singapore are not—at least, if at all, to a much less degree.

So it comes about that where the Chinese government, if so minded, could find the best reasons for intervention on behalf of its oppressed ethnic kin, it could not expect that such intervention could establish the local Chinese in authority; and where such intervention could in theory convert some countries into overseas Chinese possessions inhabited by majority or near majority Chinese communities, there is the least incentive, or excuse, for intervention to 'liberate' an oppressed people. There is no doubt that the Chinese government is aware of this paradox. There is less certainty that it helps them to formulate a coherent, or a varying policy, towards the overseas Chinese in the different countries concerned.

Malaysia at first incorporated Singapore as a constituent state in the federation. In 1965 Singapore was forced out of the federation,

and became fully independent. This event resulted in some relaxa-
tion of the extreme anti-Communist legislation which prevailed in
Malaysia; the Bank of China, a Peking controlled institution, was
reprieved from imminent closure. But diplomatic relations were not
established with China. The main opposition party to the ruling
moderate socialist party, the P.A.P. (People's Action Party), was
the Barisan Sosialis Party which, in spite of its Malay name, was in
fact run and controlled by Chinese of Communist allegiance. In
Singapore a persistent attempt has been made to keep up the
appearance, and to some degree the reality, of a multi-racial state.
Malay remains one of the official languages, indeed is mainly used
for street names and other official nomenclature, and prominent
non-Chinese occupy important offices in the government. Yet the
electorate is overwhelmingly Chinese (80 per cent) and that it is in
part strongly influenced by left-wing thinking is unquestionable.

Unlike the countries in which the Chinese form a minority mainly
engaged in trade and industry, in Singapore, and to a great degree in
Malaysia also (especially in cities like Penang or Kuala Lumpur,
where the Chinese are the majority), the Chinese community cannot
be described as a purely merchant or bourgeois class. There are both
rich and moderately well-to-do businessmen, prosperous artisans,
and a poor proletariat. In a society more nearly racially homogeneous,
social problems steadily tend to outweigh communal interests. There
is a division between the rich and the poor which does not follow
ethnic lines, and this fact in itself largely invalidates the often
expressed fear that the Chinese community as a whole could become
a 'Fifth Column' for Peking aggression. To achieve that deplorable
confrontation it would be necessary for the whole body of the Chinese
to believe that they had no future other than that of servitude under
existing regimes. The facts are very different. In Malaysia, it may
be that, following the grave communal riots of May 1969, a certain
section of the Malay population would be willing to see the enforce-
ment of discrimination against Chinese on a wider scale, comparable
to the policies of Indonesia or the Philippines; but wiser counsels
still prevail, and to men of discernment it is clear that such policies
in a country where numbers are so nearly in balance would lead to
great unrest and unpredictable dangers.

There is in any case no such possibility in Singapore. The record
of the government of Lee Kuan Yew, although not free from criticism
on other questions, has been one of scrupulously avoiding policies
which seemed to favour the majority Chinese against other, much
smaller communities. This attitude is no doubt derived from realistic
consideration of the character of the state of Singapore itself, but it
also serves as an example of how a majority Chinese community

treats its minorities, and is, hopefully, a reassurance to nervous onlookers outside. A more real cause of friction is that the progressive policies of Singapore are another kind of example to her neighbours, and not one very welcome to more conservative politicians. The opposition to the ruling P.A.P. in Singapore is in effect a concealed Communist front; it has refused to contest elections on the grounds that the results would be weighted against them, or the fear that whatever support they might get, they would be debarred from office, or perhaps, the opposite fear, that their showing might be much poorer than their pretensions. The result has been to make the government fearful of a potential insurgency if the Barisan Socialis Party came into the open, or was allowed to operate too freely. This is a barrier to closer relations with China, as the fear that a legal Communist Party would seek inspiration, if not actually accept direction, from Peking is powerful.

There is another potential difficulty, gradually appearing more real, which inhibits closer relations between Singapore and China. Singapore is developing rapidly and enjoys one of the highest standards of living of any country in Asia, not far short of that of Japan. It is, in spite of a government which professes moderate socialist objectives, a capitalist and free enterprise economy, with large scale foreign investment and considerable local capital resources. It is thus an example of the modernization and progress of a majority Chinese state on lines very different from those followed in China itself, and the evidence is that this system is not disagreeable to the majority of the inhabitants, while the benefits of better housing, and other progressive measures are widely appreciated. So far from China having any cause to 'liberate' Singapore from the oppression of a foreign, or non-Chinese domination, the possibility is rather that Singapore will provide an alternative way to modern and better living which could be attractive to Chinese in any country. It may be that in time the development of the Chinese economy, facing a far vaster task, will provide the people of China with what they will accept as the good life, or the best available, but it is also at least equally probable that Singapore will be there to exhibit a rival model. That a very large number of Chinese Singaporeans are willing to see themselves as Singaporeans first and ethnic Chinese second, and to see no irreconcilable conflict in these two characters is already apparent.

Malaysia, like Singapore, if less definitely, may be on the same road. The Chinese are a 40 per cent minority, and economically predominant. They have a role in political life, one which was restricted following the 1969 riots, but not discounted for the future. Parliamentary government inevitably involves the participation of

Chinese political parties, based on the very large Chinese electorates of the major cities of the western side of the Malay Peninsula, and also upon the 30 per cent Chinese population of Sarawak in Borneo. The exuberance with which the election results of 1969, which marked a considerable growth in the support of such parties, was greeted, was the spark which started off the riots of May in that year and led to the suspension of parliamentary government. That this was not a final solution, nor one with which the country could live for long, has been recognized by the predominantly Malay government. Their predicament was partly due to the fact that the Chinese conservative partner in the coalition, the Malayan Chinese Association, was a heavy loser in favour of Chinese parties representing less affluent classes. Here, therefore, is the same problem: the division between rich and poor begins to loom as more significant than the communal divisions on ethnic grounds.

The configuration of politics, communal strength and social divisions in Malaysia and in Singapore thus differ very greatly from the conditions found in other parts of Southeast Asia. For Peking they present a problem equally different, and just as difficult, as those posed elsewhere. Essentially, if China were to be inspired either with world-wide revolutionary zeal, as is usually believed, or by national ambitions of aggrandizement, of which there is no great evidence, the possibilities of positive action in either case depend more upon the activity of sympathizers within the countries of Southeast Asia rather than in overt operations based in China itself. The distances are very great and the U.S.A. controls the seas. In Malaysia and still more in Singapore, the incentive to work within the country for a future Chinese domination is not strong, and grows if anything weaker with passing time. The majority of the Chinese, all indeed except the ageing, are people born and reared in the country itself, for immigration on any significant scale ended in 1932, which is forty years ago. Locally born Chinese, now free to participate in local political life, have much less active interest in the politics of China than their fathers and grandfathers had, in an age when there were no local politics under colonial rule, and the future of China was a burning issue with all men of education.

On the other hand China remains the great neighbour, whose strange yet potent social experiment dominates the East Asian scene. No country can ignore it; the excuse of anti-Communism becomes less meaningful when the major anti-Communist power, America, recognizes that the time has come to face the facts and arrive at some form of co-existence. The evidence of the Cultural Revolution and its disclosures reveals that for China the Southeast Asian region is also a problem, and one for which their government has as yet no real answer. This discovery, as it seeps into the con-consciousness of political leaders and their advisers will gradually moderate fears and perhaps inspire policies less ideologically commit-ted and more in tune with inescapable facts. The Chinese regime in Peking publicly renounces the ideals of 'Great Han Chauvinism' by which they mean something very like the former Nationalist doctrine 'once a Chinese always a Chinese'. If this attitude is maintained in the wake of the Cultural Revolution and is accepted as at least valid at the present time by rulers of Southeast Asia, it could bring about an easier relationship.

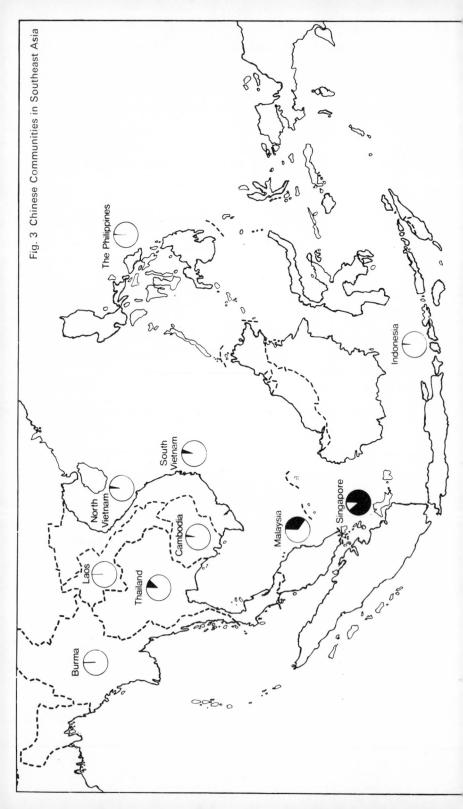

Fig. 3 Chinese Communities in Southeast Asia

Chapter Five

CHINA AND THE OVERSEAS CHINESE OF SOUTHEAST ASIA

The independent states of Southeast Asia are strictly contemporary with the Communist regime in Peking, neither older nor much younger. Both emerged from the immediate post-war situation in eastern Asia, and both were strongly antagonistic to the regimes they had succeeded or overthrown. At first the Chinese government does not seem to have appreciated these points of similarity. India, Pakistan, Burma and even Indonesia were spoken of as bogus regimes, puppets of the imperialists. It was clearly difficult for the Chinese Communists, whose own struggle had been prolonged for more than twenty years and had mainly been conducted by open warfare, to believe that imperial power could be yielded with little or no bloodshed nor independence won unless by armed struggle. The situation in Vietnam, one of China's nearest neighbours, seemed to confirm this interpretation. Indian mediation in the later stage of the Korean War, and participation in the arrangements made for the ceasefire in that war, was probably the first event to convince the Chinese Communists that the independence of the former dominions and colonies was real and valid. But it was the Bandung Conference of Asian States in 1955 which confirmed the existence of the new order.

At that conference the Chinese delegation took a conciliatory and friendly approach to the heads of states, many of whom were distinctly hostile to Communism. It was also at Bandung that Prime Minister Chou En-lai elaborated the new doctrine of China's policy towards overseas Chinese, repudiating the Nationalist reliance upon the *jus sanguinis* and declaring that China now supported the opposite doctrine, the *jus soli*. In future, that is, China would not claim that all persons of Chinese descent were automatically, by

81

virtue of this fact, able to be and actually entitled to be considered as Chinese citizens. This had been the doctrine of the Kuomintang, and one which had enountered much opposition from the colonial governments before the war.

The Chinese Communist leader now declared that the People's Republic accepted the opposite view; that persons should normally and naturally be citizens of the country in which they were born, and only claim other nationality through special procedures or in exceptional cases, such as the children of resident foreign diplomats. This would mean if accepted fully, that all Chinese born in the countries of Southeast Asia would be citizens of those countries, but immigrants who had come from China would remain Chinese citizens unless accepted for naturalization by the host country. Chou En-lai offered to sign treaties embodying these provisions with any government ruling a Chinese minority community, if the government concerned was in diplomatic relations with the People's Republic, or recognized it as the government of China. Only Indonesia took up this offer. Some countries, such as India and Pakistan, had no Chinese minority; some with large Chinese populations such as Thailand and the Philippines were hostile to China and would not recognize Peking, and some others, conspicuously Malaysia, with a large Chinese population, were not yet independent.

The Bandung initiative was not taken very seriously by many observers at that time; it was plain that Indonesia would take a long time to ratify a treaty which affected the interests and prejudices of many of her influential classes. The states opposed to Communism, Thailand and the Philippines, were unwilling to make any move towards relations with Peking; Malaysia, with the largest Chinese minority and the one which was proportionately the largest in relation to the non-Chinese peoples of the country, was still under colonial rule. Nor was there yet any firm belief in the minds of the rulers of most of these countries that the Chinese were sincere in their new policy. It was suspected to be a trick, although just how the trick was worked seemed to defy easy explanation. A major reason for failing to devine the real nature of the new Chinese policy was the obsession, very powerful at that time, with the belief in 'international Communism' as a worldwide conspiracy aimed at every non-Communist state. As such any policy brought forward by a Communist government must necessarily be noxious to the non-Communist world, and must reflect some sinister machination. It never seems to have been considered possible that such a new policy might reflect the perplexities and problems of the Communist country itself rather than a calculated subversive assault on its neighbours.

That this second situation was in great probability the real reason for China's change of policy under the Communist regime is now apparent. The overseas Chinese were a problem for the Chinese Communists. Firstly they lived beyond the political control of Peking, and were thus subjected to other influences and exhortations than those of the Communist regime's propaganda. They had their own independent and well informed press. Secondly they lived in countries where the capitalist system was operating, haltingly perhaps in some, with increasing prosperity in others. The Chinese overseas were an essential part of this system, they were in fact in most of these countries the capitalists themselves, at least in the medium range, leaving only the largest international businesses in foreign, usually Western, control. On the other hand there were among the overseas Chinese both poor and rich. The rich might be opposed to Communism, and wary of close relations with the People's Republic, but the poor were often inclined to the parties of the Left, and a very high proportion of them were either immigrants from China themselves or the sons and daughters of recent immigrants. Thus the influential overseas Chinese might not be expected to support Peking, but the poor and underprivileged might well look to Communist China as a protector.

The overseas Chinese had also an economic importance for China; they remitted home to their families and relatives in south China large sums of money, thus bringing in welcome foreign exchange. They would hardly continue this helpful practice if the funds they sent were not allowed to reach the people they wished to help. So it would be necessary to tolerate a class of people in the southern provinces who gained a steady income by receiving foreign funds, earned by capitalist enterprise abroad, and these people must be allowed to enjoy these very un-Communist amenities for fear that otherwise the supply of foreign exchange would dry up. Principles and practices were in clear conflict.

There was another problem: the Chinese in many of the countries of Southeast Asia were not a popular community with the other inhabitants. They had too clear an economic lead, they were too often in the position of creditor, money lender, and entrepreneur, and the native people in the positions of debtor, borrower and labourer. Even if the poor among the Chinese themselves had a tendency to left wing political allegiance, if not to actual Communist Party membership, this was not a very helpful attitude for the advancement of revolutionary movements in these countries. What the Chinese did, others would not follow; a movement under Chinese leadership would not gain much, or any, following from non-Chinese. But as the Chinese were in most countries a minority, the development of revolutionary zeal among them did little to promote a real revolution, but a great deal to bring down upon the Chinese community, and thus upon Communist China also, the wrath of the local regime, representing the majority of the population. Overseas Chinese who were Communists were counter-productive to a real revolutionary movement.

Thus the problem was twofold. Encouragement of the overseas Chinese well-to-do or rich, while it might continue the flow of remittances and aid the foreign exchange situation, was somewhat repugnant to Communist principles and created a social problem in China itself, among the recipients of overseas incomes. Attempts to promote revolutionary ideas among the poor overseas Chinese could very probably bear fruit, but it would be Dead Sea fruit; the more revolutionary the Chinese overseas became, the more they would be distrusted as a 'fifth column' of Peking by nationalists, and suspected by native Communists of ruining their own prospects and spoiling the chances of creating a real revolution. It is now very clear that these considerations lay behind Chou En-lai's offer at Bandung, and the new policy of *jus soli* was designed, if possible, to relieve China of an embarrassing commitment and involvement which a Communist regime is not well equipped to meet.

Chou En-lai had also stated that for those Chinese who were not eligible to naturalize under the laws of the countries in which they lived, mainly the immigrants born in China, China was ready and willing to welcome them home, where there was ample opportunity for the exercise of their skills and knowledge. This was probably a serious and realistic proposal; China, just entering at that time into the first stages of her new industrial revolution, did indeed need all the technically skilled workers she could muster, and a good proportion of the overseas Chinese fell into this category. There was also a large number of educated young people for whom the prospects abroad might seem uncertain if not actually bleak. Had there been a wider response to Chou's proposals it is at least possible that several thousands of overseas Chinese would have decided to return; but in many countries the strong anti-Communist attitudes of their governments opposed any attempt to explore or negotiate the suggestions put forward by the Chinese Prime Minister at Bandung.

Another factor which made any uniform policy difficult to apply was the wide variation in the situation and potential local influence of the overseas Chinese in different countries. In Indonesia they were an economically powerful but numerically small minority in proportion to the other peoples of the archipelago. In the Philippines they were in much the same situation, suffering discrimination and minor forms of persecution, yet even more indispensable to the economy. In Malaysia they formed a 40 per cent minority, and if the smaller Indian minority was taken into account, the two minority peoples were the equal in numbers to the Malays. In Singapore the

Chinese were in a clear and large majority. A policy which might meet the needs of the smaller minorities, even if in actual numbers these (as in Indonesia) were far from negligible, was not so suited to the countries where the Chinese were long settled and also occupied a position of nearly equal strength to the other races. An Indonesian Chinese could see no prospect of ever being allowed a real voice in the conduct of affairs in his native or adopted country, nor could his cousin in the Philippines. But in Singapore and Malaysia this prospect was real and imminent. Independence for Malaysia, as the British made plain, depended upon the prior agreement of the two major peoples of the country to work in harmony upon an agreed basis of shared power. In the decade following Bandung this agreement came about, helped by the realization that it would undermine the appeal of the Communist insurgents, and thus, by removing that problem, enable the British to withdraw.

The younger generation in Malaysia and Singapore could now look to a local future no longer confined to commerce and business enterprise, nor in these fields restricted by discriminatory legislation. No government in Malaysia has ever, before or since independence, proposed to pass legislation depriving the Chinese of the right to undertake this or that business or from engaging in any lawful occupation. But in Indonesia, the Philippines and in Thailand such laws are enforced. A Communist government might seem to have little interest in the freedom or lack of it with which capitalists may engage in various forms of free enterprise: all these activities should be, and in principle are, noxious in their view. But the facts of the situation meant in practice that Chinese policy towards the overseas Chinese had a varying impact. In the countries where the Chinese were a repressed minority, China seemed a hope, even if not an unmitigated blessing; in countries where the Chinese had in law, if not in political power, an equal standing, the attractions of the People's Republic were less apparent.

The Malaysian Chinese, and those of Singapore, were now at long last taking an active interest in the political life and future of the countries in which they lived, and in consequence, a less active interest in the affairs of their ancestral homeland, which had been their sole political interest before the Communists came to power. It was not that Chinese leaders aspired to rule others as a master race, but that they saw that the protection of the interests and liveli-hood of their own people needed the active participation in political life of the Chinese community. The terms of Chou En-lai's proposal were not therefore particularly attractive to them: those born in the country were already by British law, citizens, and had to be accepted as such after independence; those who had been born in China, a large proportion, had no wish to return to homes they had left many years previously, but did aspire to an equal status in the country where they had settled and worked for a lifetime. Immigration from China had virtually ceased in the early 1930s, a generation before the independence of Malaysia and Singapore.

Since the Cultural Revolution in China, the policy followed by the Communist regime from its inception until 1966 has come under strong attack from the purists and revolutionary minded critics which the movement brought to power. Consequently the public denunciation of these policies has for the first time fully and clearly revealed what they were, and left no doubt of their temporizing quality, a point which is the focus of the criticism directed against them. The chief architect and for eighteen years the executive head who carried out these policies was Liao Ch'eng-chih, Chairman of the Overseas Chinese Affairs Commission, the organ set up by the new regime to replace the Nationalist Ministry for Overseas Chinese. The very fact that the Communists chose a less prestigious title than 'Ministry' indicates that the Commission was not to have the standing and authority of a full Department of State. Liao based his policy on the proposition that under the new dispensation of post-colonial empires transformed into nation states, in which the Chinese population was often unpopular and suspect, the 'philosophy of survival' was the first objective. The overseas Chinese must be able to make their living, to survive as communities, to be sheltered if possible from the more outrageous forms of repression and persecution. China was not in practice (as the Malayan Emergency had clearly proved) able or willing to engage in distant and dangerous adventures to give military support to armed uprisings. Policies which would lead the overseas Chinese, or some classes of them, to expect such assistance or deliverance must be eschewed, if false hopes were not to be raised, and serious international complications avoided.

In implementation of these assessments, directives issuing from the Commission urged a repression of class struggles which would identify Chinese as leaders or active supporters of extreme left wing policies, since if they were so identified animosity against all Chinese residents would be stimulated and the possible revolutionary value of these activities would be negligible. The open and vocal identification of overseas Chinese with China on ethnic grounds was also to be deplored, as this too would exacerbate anti-Chinese feeling and breed suspicions of the 'Fifth Column' type. This policy was made explicit in China itself in documents published in 1957—ten years before the Cultural Revolution—and it is interesting to learn that the endorsement came from no lesser person than Chou En-lai himself. In 1956, when in Burma, Chou had made a speech to the overseas Chinese in Burma which stated, 'China calls on overseas compatriots to obey the laws, and respect the customs, habits and religious beliefs of the countries of residence'. Chinese were urged to intermarry with the Burmese, become Burmese citizens, and if they did so refrain from further involvement in overseas Chinese organizations. Those who retained Chinese citizenship should not take part in any political activities in the country where they resided. He stated that China did not promote the organization of Communist or democratic parties among overseas Chinese. Those who wanted to participate in political parties should return to China.

These views were therefore those of the Prime Minister of China in 1956-57.

In 1966 they were under strong criticism and attack, but Chou En-lai was not identified with them by the critics. That they formed the basis of Chinese policy until the Cultural Revolution would appear virtually established, and this explains the background to the Bandung proposals, made only one year before Chou's speech in Burma. Although it was not impossible for outside observers to learn of these policies, no account was taken of them in the press of the Western world, and it would seem, very little if any in the decision making of the governments of the countries of Southeast Asia. Yet these statements, had they been made before the war by a Nationalist Chinese Prime Minister, would have been sweet music in the ears of all colonial authorities throughout Southeast Asia. Even if they had been only partly accepted or believed it seems strange that they should not at least have been seen as a clue to the difficulties which the Chinese government faced in relations with the overseas Chinese communities. Chou En-lai was not addressing the Western press, nor the representatives of hostile governments in Southeast Asia; he was talking to the Chinese of Burma with obvious wider reference to the Chinese in all other countries of the region. Therefore what he said was expected to be believed, and followed, by his auditors.

Critics of the policies followed until 1966 also charge that the task of protecting the overseas Chinese from undue persecution was not properly or truly undertaken. In 1956 South Vietnam forced the Chinese minority, mainly concentrated in the Saigon suburb of Cholon, to naturalize as Vietnamese, with a view to imposing military conscription upon them. It is charged that Liao Ch'eng-chih did not protest against this action for a full year, and that when he did so the protest was couched in mild terms, and was unavailing. Yet South Vietnam was a militant anti-Communist state already at that time entering into the early stages of the long conflict with North Vietnam and the Liberation Front of South Vietnam, a conflict in which China's policy has consistently given support to the opponents in Saigon.

No question has evoked more passion and concern than education amongst the overseas Chinese. The communities established their own schools, and maintained them, at a time when no colonial government was willing to do anything for the education of the local Chinese youth. Later, the realization that Chinese schools had a strong ethnic bias, were staffed by teachers brought from China, used Chinese textbooks and were becoming the foci for Nationalist propaganda, aroused the attention and concern of the colonial authorities, and after independence of the new governments in power. The Nationalist Chinese government had made education in Chinese culture a major point in their overseas Chinese policy. They saw it as the vital factor which would keep the Chinese spiritually, and indeed politically also, loyal to the homeland. If Chinese youth was taught in foreign tongues and learned to read only foreign literature, their Chinese character would disappear, and they would be assimilated, without even acquiring the full benefits of a new nationality.

The argument may, in point of fact, be questioned on the varied experience of many other parts of the world. The Irish have, except for a tiny minority, long since lost their ancestral Gaelic speech, but certainly not their sense of national identity. The French Canadians, on the other hand, have retained the language of their ancestors but do not in any real sense identify with France in any other way. The same phenomenon is to be observed in South America, and it is at least very probable that in Rhodesia we shall soon see the emergence of an English speaking, Anglo-Saxon descended community which repudiates any national connection with its ancestral homeland. Ethnic Chinese who no longer could speak or read Chinese, could on these analogies remain a distinct people; ethnic Chinese who retained their language could equally be citizens of a country which had no political ties with China.

The Chinese Communists, whether taking these examples into account or not, dropped the Nationalist support for Chinese education amongst the overseas Chinese. Schools were urged to teach the local language and culture, and even to adopt the local language as the medium for instruction. Specific accusations against Liao Ch'eng-chih made during the Cultural Revolution attest that this was his policy (and that of the Chinese government) during the first fifteen years of the Chinese People's Republic. There were obvious reasons for doing so: China was a Communist state; in her own territory all education was therefore orientated towards the social and econom-ic teaching of Marx, Lenin and Mao Tse-tung. The overseas Chinese schools had in pre-Communist days imported both textbooks and teachers from China, and their instruction had been closely modelled on the patterns used in China, approved by the Ministry of Education of the Nationalist government in Nanking. Had such practices continued, the consequences now that China was under a Communist government would have been disastrous. No government in Southeast Asia would have accepted Communist trained teachers, Communist slanted textbooks and instruction generally on Communist lines. Most of these governments were in actual conflict with their own Communist parties or movements, and some were extremely hostile to all publication of Communist literature however well known or theoretical. The adoption of the Nationalist policy would have led to the immediate closing of all Chinese schools, and great difficulties in getting them reopened.

Another aspect of the policy of Liao and his colleagues concerned the question of repatriation of Chinese who either had no hope of continuing to make a living overseas, or who were virtually threatened with deportation by discriminatory laws. This problem mainly concerned Indonesia. As had been hinted in Chou En-lai's Bandung proposals, China declared herself willing to take back all who were forced to leave, or desired to return. After Indonesia had suppressed the Chinese rural traders and destroyed their livelihood this problem became urgent. Liao Ch'eng-chih was accused in the Cultural Revolution of not only failing to mobilize the persecuted Chinese to wage mass self-defence struggles, but also for suggesting that the best policy was to repatriate some 600,000 Chinese affected by the new Indonesian discriminatory laws. He is also said to have suggested that three to five million overseas Chinese should be repatriated over a period of seven to eight years from various foreign countries. Presumably these numbers would mainly be made up from Chinese who had emigrated to Southeast Asia, and who could not obtain local citizenship under the laws of those countries.

In the event no such ambitious programme proved feasible; the numbers were scaled down, and obstruction (strangely enough) from the Indonesian authorities prevented all but a relatively small number returning to China. The fact remains that the official policy of the Peking government during the years between 1955 and 1966 was to repatriate very large numbers of overseas Chinese, and that it was the physical obstacles and political obstruction of foreign governments rather than any lack of intention in China which largely frustrated this programme.

These facts constitute proof that the policy of Peking was to disengage from the problems of the overseas Chinese; to urge those that could to assimilate and naturalize where they lived, and for those to whom these choices were not open, to aid their return to China. The policy was the direct opposite of that of the Nationalist regime when in power in China. Once again, far from recognizing and welcoming this change, the governments of almost all Southeast Asian countries either ignored it, or obstructed it. Perhaps realization that the elimination or major reduction of the Chinese minorities would seriously damage economies already very weak, or fears that they might be expected to bear some share of the high cost of repatriating such large numbers, deterred them. It is however, hardly logical to complain of the presence and activity of Chinese minorities and at the same time obstruct policy which would lead to their removal.

This then was the policy, and its results, of the Chinese government from about 1954, when it was formed, until 1966 when the Cultural Revolution exposed it to violent criticism. It applied to all overseas Chinese, and no explicit exception was made between the countries where Chinese were a small minority and Malaysia where they were a very large one. Repatriation was never an issue in Malaysia; it does not appear to have affected the Philippines or Thailand, countries which refuse all relations with China and are thereby debarred from negotiating any agreements with the government in Peking. In practice the repatriation policy only applied to Indonesia, whose government had diplomatic relations with China, which before the fall of Sukarno were close. Even there it effected very little. In Burma, where the Chinese community is relatively small, it was never invoked. The large scale proposals attributed to Liao Ch'eng-chih were never within sight of realization, and the policy of China towards the overseas Chinese before the Cultural Revolution must be adjudged hesitant, indecisive, timid and inconclusive. This is not the picture of the new China which the regime was anxious to display, and it was not the image of 'Red China' which the anti-Communist world was willing to entertain; consequently there was an involuntary but effective co-operation from both sides to obscure the facts.

The Cultural Revolution has revealed them. The critics, Red Guards and their news-sheets, have bitterly criticized the Overseas Chinese Affairs Commission for 'revisionist' policies and lack of revolutionary zeal. The criticisms seem just: the policy followed was certainly not one which encouraged overseas Chinese participation in local revolutionary movements, and, since it condoned or even encouraged overseas Chinese continuing to operate their 'capitalist' businesses, may also be categorized as 'revisionist'. Liao Ch'eng-chih was driven from office in July 1967; the Overseas Chinese Affairs Commission virtually ceased operations from that

time, if it has not been formally abolished. In September 1966 its
Shanghai office was assaulted and overrun by Red Guards. But no
new policy has emerged; the whole question of overseas Chinese
affairs has dropped into limbo, there has been no policy at all since
1966, and the only statements made have been to the effect that
China has always counselled overseas Chinese to conform to the
laws of the country in which they live. Repatriation has virtually
ceased, and although the enthusiasm for Mao Tse-tung, and the
wearing of Mao badges provoked riots in Burma in 1967 which led to
a sharp change in the hitherto good relations between China and
Burma, there has been since 1969 some attempt to mend these fences.

It would seem that since the Cultural Revolution China has ceased
to concern herself with her overseas kith and kin; the past policies
were a useful stick with which to beat out of office some of the Party
hierarchs who could be accused of revisionism, but the critics did not
formulate any alternative policy. The problem still exists; the
overseas Chinese remain in very large numbers, and their difficulties
have not diminished. The Malaysian riots of 1969 have, if anything,
shown that even in the most hopeful environment the risk of communal strife is real, and the danger that Chinese political rights will
be impaired or destroyed is ever present. But China has taken no
action in respect of this situation. Liao's policy may be derided,
but seems to be followed in practice. The new turn of social policy
in China makes the assimilation of returned Chinese more difficult
than before, and the erosion of time and family connections, so long
interrupted, has led to a constant decrease in the remittance of funds
from abroad. The economic motive for support for the overseas
Chinese is diminishing and must disappear as the years pass. On the
other hand the persistance of discrimination both political and in
some countries still more powerfully in economic matters must if
anything, reinforce the overseas Chinese sense of danger and their
aspirations for a 'liberation'. China may wish to disembarrass herself
of a difficult problem; those who constitute the problem may be
forced by discrimination and persecution to seek to re-engage China.

The problem for the Southeast Asian countries is twofold; they
seek to modernize, and on the whole, with modifications, attempt this
process through the operation of the capitalist system. Involved as
they are in that world which the West dominates, they have no
alternative short of Communist revolution. But in their countries
the native capitalists are in effect overwhelmingly the Chinese
resident community; no attempts to create an alternative capitalist
class have met with any success. If the capitalists are to be persecuted because they are Chinese, and the poorer overseas Chinese
suspected of Communist sympathies, then no accomodation with

either class is likely to last. Capitalism without the co-operation and free activity of local capitalists must only result in the control of the economy by foreign interests, a prospect which all these countries deplore; antagonism to Chinese as such must sooner or later rouse the hostility of China herself, a force which will increasingly count in the affairs of Southeast Asia. The hitherto moderate policy of the People's Republic was ignored or suspected, and evoked no co-operation. It is hardly likely that some new and more aggressive policy which might emerge from the Cultural Revolution will be more welcome in Southeast Asia.

Under Liao Ch'eng-chih the Chinese policy did not favour treating Chinese communities overseas as minority peoples; it was considered undesirable that they should acquire the position of a distinct nation in the countries of their residence; the alternatives favoured were assimilation or repatriation. The local governments and the social pressures to which they respond have made the first alternative virtually unattainable; the second alternative broke down from the sheer physical scale of the proposed solution and the inability or unwillingness of the parties concerned to finance it. Thus, in the end the Chinese overseas do seem destined to become local minority nations, and whether they continue to speak Chinese and be educated in Chinese culture or in the local language is, as other examples prove, largely irrelevant.

In Indonesia, Thailand and the Philippines the acquisition of the local nationality, whether by birth or naturalization still leaves the Chinese under political and often economic disabilities. They are not equal citizens; therefore they are being turned into a peculiar people, one which cannot be eliminated, but will not be accorded equal status. This is not a treatment, as much history shows, which is likely to lead to harmony and content. In Malaysia, the Chinese are too numerous a minority to submit to this solution; and in fact in Sarawak they are the largest single race. In Singapore, they form the strong majority. In all these countries there is a minority of Chinese who are supporters of the (usually banned) Communist Parties. But they are not a majority, and the greater number would prefer to find alternative modes of political allegiance. The fact that some Communist Parties in these countries are largely recruited from Chinese does not necessarily mean that they are organized or financed from Peking. The evidence is rather to the contrary.

The example of China is potent, and to all Chinese at least, fascinating, often winning a somewhat grudging admiration. The Communists have made China strong and feared, if not loved abroad. No previous regime in China since the eighteenth century has achieved this restoration of power. It is inevitable that ardent reformers, conscious of the disabilities under which they and their kinsmen suffer, should look to China and if inclined to the Communist solution, see China as the great example and mentor. Peking cannot avoid the consequences of its own prestige and reputation. The Chinese have a deep pride in their own cultural achievement over the centuries; their arrival at the level of literate and artistic civilization, and the organization of durable and strong political power long preceded, by many centuries, any such achievement in the countries of Southeast Asia. Such a heritage is not easily forgotten, and cannot be ignored. For the first hundred years or more the overseas Chinese were mainly poor, illiterate and ignorant; then they began to acquire wealth, and immediately, in consonance with the traditions of their nation, devoted their money to the building up of educational institutions for their own community. They are now as informed, as well educated, and more in touch with the outside world than their compatriots in China itself. They are no longer a people of transient coolies working to save enough money to go home to the south China village. Policies which take no account of these changes in social and educational levels are wholly unrealistic.

Now that the Cultural Revolution is concluded, or stabilized, diplomatic activity has shown that China once more seeks to implement a foreign policy but it is not entirely clear with what aims in view. The declared aims of propaganda are not necessarily those of high policy calculated for immediately attainable objectives. World Revolution is a slogan, like the early Christian belief in the imminence of the Second Coming and the end of the world. Everyone pays tribute to this belief, few act upon it. The facts of international politics pose other problems: the domination of the Pacific Ocean by the U.S.A., the contest with Russia for the leadership of the Communist world, the possible total withdrawal, over the years, of American military power from the mainland of Asia, the possible emergence of Japan once more as a major political and military force in East Asia. It is into this framework of real issues that China must fit her policy towards the countries of Southeast Asia and their resident Chinese communities. It would seem that however much the former policy and its makers may have been criticized, no easy alternative is available to men of judgement and responsibility. China is not yet equipped with the naval and air power to mount overseas interventions, and therefore cannot give effective support to Communist insurrections, whether Chinese manned or native, in the countries of Southeast Asia. China's inability to save the Indonesian Communist Party in 1965 is clear evidence of this.

To proclaim an intransigent policy of Communist subversion and ethnic allegiance to the overseas Chinese would only result in the intensification of the discrimination practised against them, and the worsening of their relations with non-Chinese peoples, even where these are tolerable. To refrain from having any active policy at all may not avail to disengage China from the problem, since it could lead to an active movement among the overseas Chinese to invoke Chinese help in their difficulties. It may be that some alternative between these extremes will be found, but it will be a difficult line and will probably be as much distrusted and misunderstood as the policy which the critics attacked in the Cultural Revolution, and which indeed, yielded only very meagre results.

The essential fact to bear in mind in considering this complicated question is that it is a major problem for China herself, not only for the countries and governments of Southeast Asia. It is a problem which will not disappear merely because the Chinese government has no answer to it, and the Southeast Asian countries dislike it; it has to be solved, and in view of the size, strength and durability of China, it cannot be solved without her co-operation and consent.

Chapter Six

SOME PROSPECTS AND CONCLUSIONS

The lessons of China's relationship with the countries of Southeast Asia since the end of the Second World War seem often to point to the opposite conclusion to that expected or assumed by Western statesmen in the past twenty years. The 'Domino Theory' has proved a fallacy; the greater the outside pressure upon China, the 'containment' policy, the more was China stimulated by traditional fear of Western aggression to expand her influence so as to forestall or frustrate that of the powerful nation, the United States, which had shown such clear signs of hostility. It may be possible that if that mistaken policy is now abandoned and pressure upon China relaxed, there will be less strong incentive to counter the Western power in every country where it seems vulnerable. The Domino Theory has proved to work, if at all, in reverse. In order to save a dubious and shaky regime hastily improvised upon the departure of the French from Saigon, the whole of Vietnam has been devastated by a destructive war. To save Cambodia, an invasion was mounted which has resulted in that once peaceful and relatively prosperous country being reduced to misery, war, and destruction. Laos has shared a like fate. But China, the alleged objective of all this assault and violence, has never had a man engaged in the war nor suffered any attack upon her own territory. The alleged protection from Communism of relatively insignificant nations at such cost, while leaving the main stronghold of Asian Communism immune and stronger than before, is surely the outstanding example of false policy in our age.

Time has exposed it; China is now, or very soon will be, a Great Power in the full meaning of that term, which now implies the control of a nuclear armoury. The U.S.S.R., by proposing a conference on the limitation of nuclear weapons to which the four earlier nuclear powers, U.S.A., U.S.S.R., Britain and France should now invite China, proves that the Russians, in spite of their continuing ideological dispute with China, recognize the need to admit her status. The U.S.A. has also seen the facts, which had long been acknowledged both in Britain and in France. Whether the acceptance of the coming of China to the nuclear group of major powers will result in any valuable limitation of such arms is uncertain, but there are other probably more immediately significant consequences of the new policies to which the major powers are groping. On 25 October 1971 the Peking government obtained a majority vote in the United Nations Assembly recognizing it as the legitimate regime entitled to China's seat at the United Nations. This involved the expulsion of the Nationalist delegation from Taiwan, and far reaching diplomatic repercussions. Nations such as Italy, where the influence of the Vatican was formerly exercised to obstruct recognition of the Peking government, have now established diplomatic relations; and nations such as Australia, where local political advantage entrenched an unyielding opposition to any recognition of Peking, have been shaken abruptly out of this complacent and provincial attitude. The effect of these changes, of this rapid movement of reappraisal, upon the neighbouring nations of Southeast Asia has not been so conspicuous.

They are closer to China; a change of policy which to Italy is a diplomatic convenience and a possible trade benefit, or to Canada serves both that purpose and the always popular move of doing something different from the U.S.A., is much more significant for small neighbouring nations, many of which have large Chinese minority populations. Recognition by the Philippines or by Thailand would be very far reaching decisions with effects not by any means confined to foreign relations. Indonesia, which had recognized China, but is now in a state of aloof and very cool relations with Peking—and is also much the largest and most populous country of Southeast Asia—could afford to return, gradually, to better relations without needing to make a dramatic gesture. Indonesian policy has carefully kept the nation clear of involvement with Western military action; there are no foreign bases in Indonesia. Consequently there are no insuperable obstacles to smoother relations with China, and there are indications that the government in Djakarta is cautiously seeking such a solution within the difficult context of its internal extreme anti-Communist policy.

One consequence of the recognition that China can no longer be ignored, will be that sooner or later, and probably sooner, it will be necessary to admit that China, like all other Great Powers, has her natural sphere of influence, or protective screen of small and friendly

powers. No one disputes the interpretation of the Monroe Doctrine
which now gives the U.S.A. a predominant role in the Caribbean
(except Cuba) and a degree of influence in the rest of South America
which is uncontested. No one, equally, however much it is distasteful
to many, can now deny that the Soviet Union exercises a similar,
indeed a much more obvious and compulsive influence in Eastern
Europe. The submission of Czechoslovakia to Russian pressure had
to be accepted, just as Guatemala was not permitted to have a left
wing, probably pro-Communist regime. The pressure upon the
Czechs may be, and does seem to Europeans, far worse than the
constraint upon the Guatemalans, but in terms of Great Power
policies it is not so dissimilar. Britain and France formerly had
similar spheres of authority in western and southern Europe; these
spheres have become merged in the evolving pattern of western
European unity, but they are sufficiently real to inspire the determination that the influence of the U.S.S.R. should stop at the western
border of the East German state, and should not penetrate to Greece.

In the earlier period of Great Power domination of Europe the
Balkan peninsula, as it emerged from Turkish rule, became a cockpit
for the rivalries of the powers. No one of them occupied a geographical position which incontestably made it the natural overlord of the
region; Germany, Austria, and Russia were all within striking range
or not far off, but none of them could claim an exclusive interest.
Britain and France, and later Italy also, could and did play their
part as powers with maritime interests or involvements in the
Mediterranean which made them also possible heirs to the failing
Turkish empire. The result first of all was local wars in which the
Great Powers backed their champions without themselves becoming
actually involved, and when this activity merely enhanced rivalries
and increased instability, the inevitable result was the assassination
at Sarajevo and the First World War. The Balkan kingdoms, distracted by local enmities and Great Power intrigues as they were, had at
least one advantage over the prospective 'Balkans' of Southeast
Asia: they had no large resident minorities of ethnic stock identical
with the citizens of one or other of the Great Powers. There were
no large settlements of Germans, Russians, or others. The contest
was not for the liberation of oppressed minorities (except locally,
where each state oppressed the minority of its neighbour's race
resident within its boundaries), but for great strategic objectives:
the German dream of a land route to the Middle East, the Russian
dream of a sea route through the Dardanelles to the warm waters of
the Mediterranean, the Austrian belief that the development of local
nationalisms in the Balkans would undermine the loyalty of the
kindred peoples who were subjects of the Dual Monarchy.

It is unfortunate, but true, that many of these features of Balkan politics before the First World War reappear in the situation of Southeast Asia today. The late colonial empires play the role of the old Turkish empire, from whose regimes the new nations have been emancipated, still cherishing the rivalries and animosities towards each other which they nourished and exhibited up to the day of their annexation by Western nations. Thailand still feels towards Burma on the one side and Cambodia on the other, just as the kings of the eighteenth century felt towards their rivals to the west and east, and the feelings are reciprocated. The internal enmities among the peoples of Indonesia are uneasily kept in check only by the superior power of the government located in the most populous island, Java. The strife between Muslim in the south and Christian Filipinos, which the Americans found hard to quell when they took the country from Spain, still glows unquenched. Malays are conscious that across the border in Thailand is a population Malay in speech and Muslim in religion, which was not many years ago organized in small sultanates in no way differing from those which now form the federation of Malaysia. Some of the Malay Peninsula sultans were themselves tributary to the king in Bangkok until this suzerainty was by various treaties transferred to the British Crown. In all these countries differences of race, language and often of religion also accentuate inherited fears and prejudices. Even the scripts in use, derived from Arabic in Muslim countries, and from Sanskrit and Pali in the Buddhist ones (but varying very considerably within this range), make intercommunication easier in the languages of the former colonial rulers than in those of the new states themselves. One may observe that this was also true in some degree in the Balkans. French was a wider medium of communication than any local language, and Turkish was still used by the older generation.

Culturally individual, politically weak, ethnically much divided, and in religion of opposing faiths, the peoples of Southeast Asia have few links between themselves. But there is one, which was not present in the Balkans. The economic life of each of these countries is in effect largely in the hands of the immigrant, but now long settled Chinese community. In the Balkans it was the Jews who played this role, with equal ability to transcend frontiers and bestride cultures, since they had their own. But the Jews were not ethnic kin to the people of one of the Great Powers of the region: the Chinese of Southeast Asia are Chinese; and China is not far away. If Southeast Asia has become the Balkan peninsula of Asia, and has many characteristics qualifying it for that ominous analogy, one may observe in the attitudes of the Great Powers a similar analogy with the policies of the European Powers in the pre-1914 Balkan States.

The main difference is that more of the Great Powers are distant overseas nations with local interests—like Britain and France in the Balkans—and only one, China, is a nearby contiguous land power. This fact underlines another aspect: Britain and France did not in the end decide the final fate of the Balkan nations; it was the contest of the great land powers, Russia and Germany (having incorporated Austria), which settled the matter in favour of Russia, and the Communist regimes which she put into power, or which, as in Yugoslavia, modelled themselves on ideas derived from Russia. Only Greece, almost immune from direct land pressure and largely an island state, could be ultimately kept outside the Russian sphere of power. The possibility of a similar solution emerging in Southeast Asia, by which the Americans and their Western allies are able to maintain their influence over regimes situated in island countries, but must renounce the mainland to the land power, can hardly be seen as unrealistic.

There is no certain fatality about international relations and policies. No problem is ever truly solved, it simply changes, fades away, or becomes part of a wider context. The clear cut confrontation of China, the U.S.A. and the Soviet Union, with their array of allies and clients, which seemed so evident only a few years ago, has already undergone significant modification. China and Russia, at first close allies, then acutely disagreeing, now seem once more to be moving towards toleration, if not to friendship. The U.S.A. modifies her rooted opposition to China; Britain virtually resigns her residual interest in the east of Asia; and Australia gradually awakens to the consequences of these changes. In Southeast Asia the realization of the fact of the new powerful China and the impermanence of military strength based only on sea power is causing the nations of the region to explore the possibility of closer co-operation, but still dividing them as to whether this should be directed against Chinese influence, or seek to accommodate with it. The Balkan history can be a warning; it need not be a model for the future. Part of the warning which should be heeded is that it was the jealousies and enmities of the Balkan peoples themselves, their readiness to inflict on each other all the injustices they had in common suffered under Turkish rule, which gave the outside Great Powers the excuse and the opportunities for intervention, and a rivalry which ultimately brought about catastrophe.

Whether the Balkan example is avoided or not the situation of China makes the region of Southeast Asia the natural area for her influence. The north is for China not an open road. Beyond her northern frontiers lies the U.S.S.R., so that for China the presence of Russia is an irremovable fact just as China herself is one for the nations of Southeast Asia. Russia will not disappear, and the territories, once part of the Manchu Empire which the Tsars annexed a hundred years ago, are now settled with Russian people. Within the northern frontiers of the Chinese People's Republic, in Manchuria, Inner Mongolia, and Sinkiang, the great northwestern province, there are rich resources and ample land which can be utilized with modern techniques. China has no real need to seek expansion into Siberia. But the economies of the southern countries of Asia, within the tropical zone, produce many things of which China, like other industrial nations is in need, and for which the need will grow. Whether influence is exerted by political or economic pressures it is certain that China cannot do without the countries of Southeast Asia.

If it were to be conceded that China's national interest and her status as a Great Power require that she exercise in this region the same degree of overall authority and influence which the U.S.A. and the Soviet Union claim in the regions contiguous to their homelands, and see as vital to their strategic defence, it may be asked what would be the consequences of such a concession. On the analogy of policy towards Burma and to Cambodia under Prince Sihanouk, what China essentially would require is neutrality, strict and unwavering. No foreign military presence, no foreign bases. It is not at all certain on the evidence that China would require a Communist regime in power. No such demand was made on Burma, nor upon Cambodia. Revolution, the Chinese hold, cannot be exported; it must be home grown. This does not mean that it must not be favoured, encouraged, and if successful, recognized. The Russians have not invariably insisted that all their neighbours must have Communist regimes. Finland is a conspicuous example to the contrary, and no other nation lies so close to important regions of the U.S.S.R. as Finland. But the limits within which Finland may operate her democratic free society are clearly understood; no foreign alliance, no foreign bases. The Communist Party is legal and can compete for the votes of all citizens. China could, very possibly would, be ready to see 'Finlands' in Southeast Asia. Singapore could be an obvious candidate.

Such a solution would in any case be preferable to the Balkanization of Southeast Asia and the consequent wars and devastations, ending inevitably in a major clash between the Great Powers, with infinitely more serious consequences than the wars of 1914 and 1939. To arrive at such a solution peacefully requires changes of policy on both sides. The Chinese must reassure their neighbours and the more distant powers that better relations do not entail either concealed intervention in favour of a local revolution, nor overt plans of aggrandisement. It must be said that when the Chinese have endeavoured, as at Bandung, to put this message, it has not been received or understood. The Great Powers of the West must also recognize that they cannot deny to China the authority and influence which they feel themselves entitled to exercise in their own spheres. Great Power status may not be ethically altogether admirable, nor ideally desirable in a better world, but it is with us now, it is the reality of international society. To claim that because it is not a perfect system, we should enjoy it, but others must not aspire to it, is hardly a credible or presentable argument.

The nations of Southeast Asia must also make their contribution; so far they have not done very much to bring about better relations. Of all the nations considered in this study only three entered into diplomatic relations with China: Indonesia, Burma, and Cambodia. Indonesia has withdrawn to a minimal contact with China, only just short of breaking off relations; Burma, after a long period of good relations, was offended by the local exuberance of the Cultural Revolution, and has been cautious about renewing former ties. Cambodia, by the revolution which drove out Prince Sihanouk, was forced out of neutrality and her new regime has broken relations with China, which continues to recognize Sihanouk as the legitimate ruler. Thailand, South Vietnam, and the Philippines have eschewed any formal relations with China of any kind, and Malaysia and Singapore have in practice followed a similar policy. It would seem inevitable, and desirable, that these policies be changed, and as soon as practicable. Thailand and Malaysia have responded to the changing situation by tentative moves to explore the possibilities of a change of policy. It seems probable that in Indonesia there are influential people who wish to act in the same way, and even in the Philippines, Foreign Minister Romulo, long known as a doughty opponent of Communism and China, has publicly called for more realism in the presentation of news from China. More realism in the news could well be the forerunner of more prudence in foreign policy.

If the problem was only that China had once more become the major power in East Asia, the position she occupied for many centuries, these adjustments would be relatively easy. But the situation is not so simple. China is not only a new Great Power, she is the exponent of a new version of the Communist doctrine, which she claims is the true one, free from the revisionism with which the Russian brand is 'tainted'. What China preaches all Communist Parties should practice. But the revisionist 'heresy' with which Russia is besmirched is, in the eyes of many non-Communist observers the very aspect of Soviet society which they find most reassuring. Russia seems to be slowly, with many hitches, moving towards a more 'liberal' society and government. World Revolution is not preached with much fervour, Russian national interests are seen as coming first. Russia controls her external 'empire' with more open force than America exercises towards mildly recalcitrant allies or clients, but these are Great Power characteristics, not revolutionary ideology in action. Russian naval operations in the Mediterranean or the Indian Ocean are new, but not unfamiliar activities for a Great Power; so long as they do not become involved in the support of Communist revolution, they are, because they must be, acceptable if unwelcome to other powers. There is in fact to some degree a measure of counter-revolutionary value in the open pursuit of Russian national interests. Many Communists in other countries were shocked and disillusioned by the invasion of Czechoslovakia. Many Communists in Asia might well ask why the Egyptian Party remained banned and persecuted while Russia armed and equipped the government which oppressed them. The Chinese are quick to point out these marks of the revisionist beast.

In Southeast Asia the message of the Cultural Revolution is far from clear; on the one hand it is an internal Chinese reconstruction of the Party and the system of government; but it is also a new ideology which claims to reform the character of mankind, free men from selfishness and self-seeking careerism, and dedicate its followers to the upholding of pure revolutionary doctrine. Even among the Communist Parties, in and out of power in Southeast Asia, the Cultural Revolution has so far found no imitators. The North Vietnamese have a desperate war on their hands; the North Korean regime has its own leader, Kim Il Sung, who bows to no one. Parties in less established situations cannot afford to risk division and faction by engaging in this sort of ideological reformation. The peoples of the Southeast Asian countries may thus rightly ask what sort of China they are urged to accommodate with, and what any such relationship may imply. Russia is criticized for following national interest at the expense of ideological zeal. Her policy is called 'Socialist Imperialism'—a strange hybrid. It could therefore be supposed that China will not follow this type of policy; there will be no 'Great Han Chauvinism'—too close to 'Socialist Imperialism'— and this may be a reassurance to nervous nationalists in Southeast Asia.

But the policy makers of the first Communist period, denounced during the Cultural Revolution, were those who had followed moderate courses intended to avoid provoking national resentment against the overseas Chinese Communities. They did not have very great success in this endeavour, and that may be one reason why they were denounced. But if they were wrong, what is now deemed right? What will be the new policy, if there is to be one? As has been said in an earlier chapter, it is not possible to answer this question at the present time. Yet it is the essential question which governments in the Southeast Asian countries must ask when framing new policies towards China.

The Chinese have always appreciated the advantage of waiting until they could take the initiative at a chosen moment. The exercise of ping-pong diplomacy was an instance in point. They need not yet feel that it is for them to make the first move; nor to explain themselves to an audience which has hitherto shown only a very limited capacity to listen or to understand. Let the nations who seek to change their policies towards China come forward with their proposals, and they will be considered; from the results of that consideration the character of new Chinese policy will become apparent; and if a suitable moment occurs, will be dramatized by some headline catching action such as the invitation to an American team to play ping-pong in Peking.

The end of the Vietnam War, following the withdrawal by the Americans, will mark also the end of an era in eastern Asia. It is highly improbable that any future U.S. administration will again commit massive forces to a land war in Asia. Whether the War ends in the fall of the Saigon government, or some rather precarious compromise with a more moderate version of that regime, it will be in effect the end of the Western intervention in the affairs of mainland Asia. Henceforward the main contestants will be the Asian peoples themselves, and it is not at all certain that they will line up in the way expected of them in the West. It is not to be assumed that the evacuation of Vietnam will deeply effect the American position in the southwest Pacific. Even if China became the immediate beneficiary from the American withdrawal, she has no real naval power, and only a limited and short range air strength. The U.S. can continue to rule the eastern seas whoever rules the continent. Moreover, in that task, keeping the island nations within the non-Communist world, the U.S. will have at least the passive help of Japan. The Japanese had always strong reservations about the wisdom of the Vietnamese War. Once bitten, twice shy: they had their memories of the guerrilla war in China. But when it comes to any risk of the island world falling under the influence of either Russia or China, the Japanese are much more sensitive. There can emerge a balance between Chinese power on the mainland and American power on the seas. Russia, also a land power, but with her main strength far away, and a potential power by sea, founded on remote bases, could be a third party seeking to profit from the confrontation of the others, or use her weight, first this way, then that as circumstances demanded.

There remains one further open possibility. In the fifteenth century, about a century or less before Vasco da Gama rounded the Cape and opened up the eastern seas to European enterprise and ultimate empire, the Chinese under the early Ming dynasty had created an impressive naval power which ranged over the whole southwest Pacific, and the Indian Ocean to the coasts of Africa and Arabia. They later, for internal reasons, gave this policy up, allowed the fleet to decay, and never revived their sea power. But there is no reason why they should not do so if they choose to allocate the resources over a sufficient period of time. China produces a hardy, seafaring population well accustomed to service in merchant ships under many flags in all parts of the world. She has the ports and the technical ability to build modern warships. If she has so far done so only to a very limited degree, it is clearly because other armaments and other enterprises were given priority. This in itself is a comment upon the pervasive fears of Chinese aggression so often aired in many of the lands to her south, not excluding Australia. China simply does not now have the naval nor the air power to mount any sort of overseas invasion. When she develops such strength, as she can do at her choice, the situation in the South China Sea will resemble that coming into being with the development of Soviet naval power in the Indian Ocean: an intrusion of a power long absent, or never previously present, into an area where other powers were formerly unchallenged. It will give a new force to the Chinese claim to be the Great Power of eastern Asia; whether it will be seen as a mortal challenge by other powers cannot now be predicted.

At the meeting of the Assembly of the United Nations in September and October 1971, the Albanian sponsored resolution for the recognition of the Peking government as the sole legitimate government of China, and thus the only regime entitled to China's seat at the United Nations, was carried by a large majority, in spite of the opposition of the U.S. Chief Delegate, Mr Bush, who had endeavoured to mobilize support for an alternative resolution which would have admitted the Peking regime, but retained the concurrent membership of the Nationalist government. At the very same time Dr Kissinger, the special envoy of President Nixon, was in Peking making arrangements for the visit of President Nixon to China, a visit which had been arranged by Dr Kissinger on a previous secret mission to Peking. It is hardly surprising that in these circumstances many member governments concluded that the activities of Dr Kissinger were more indicative of real American policy than the protests and manoeuvres of Mr Bush. It would be unrealistic to doubt this assessment.

It is well known that Peking would not take any seat offered on terms which included the retention of a Nationalist delegation in the United Nations. This would be the 'Two Chinas' solution, which had been adamantly rejected not only by Peking, but also by the Nationalist government itself. Consequently the U.S. Administration knew that to succeed in retaining Taiwan in the U.N. meant excluding Peking, a position inconsistent with the policy which had sent Dr Kissinger to China. It was not difficult to conclude that the search for a better relationship with Peking was reckoned more important than the gratification of Taiwan.

The nations of Southeast Asia can, and must, read these signs. They were quickly noted by the Communist regime in North Vietnam, which promptly sought, and obtained, reassurances from China that these moves did not portend a change of policy, or a betrayal, as the Vietnamese have feared ever since they were pressured into signing the accords at Geneva which brought the war with France to an end in 1954. Among the non-Communist nations there have also already been some clear repercussions. A political change in Thailand suppressed the rather minimal democratic institutions which had recently been permitted to operate. A firm and fully military dictatorship was once more established. If this seems to be a reaction from the Right, fearing the influence of China, and doubting the continuance of American commitment in Southeast Asia, the reaction elsewhere seems to have been more a nervous realization that previous aloof and hostile attitudes to China had now become unwise. Several nations of Southeast Asia did in fact vote for the resolution seating Peking, even though they did not have diplomatic relations with that government.

In a rapidly changing international scene all prediction is close to mere speculation. Technological changes also alter the normal constants of strategy within a short time. The pattern which seems to be discernible now may well prove far from accurate, or wildly distorted within a few years' time. A quarter of a century is but a brief span in the life of nations, and the value of any assessment of China's relations with the nations of Southeast Asia since the Second World War must be considered within this passing context.

INDEX

America, United States of, relations with China, 18, 64, 74, 93, 99, 103–5; relations with Indonesia, 51; relations with the Philippines, 66, 68; war in Vietnam, 6, 13–32, 95–6, 103

Amoy, Chinese port, 36

Annam, old Chinese name for Vietnam, 8

Australia, relations with China, 96, 104; relations with Southeast Asia, 6, 99

Balkan States, analogy with Southeast Asia, 97–101

Bandung, Conference of Asian states, 27, 35, 40, 41, 42, 44, 45, 81, 82, 85, 87, 101

Bangkok, capital of Thailand, 62, 63, 98

Bao Dai, Emperor of Vietnam, 10, 11, 15

Bhamo, town in Burma, 54

Borneo, Chinese community in, 36, 42

Britain, (U.K.), recognition of People's Republic of China, 70–1; relations with Southeast Asia, 6, 14, 46, 51, 99; rule in Burma, 54, 56–60; rule in Malaysia and Singapore, 42, 68–75, 85

Buddhism, in Burma, 56; in India, 3; in Thailand, 62

Burma, Chinese community in, 56, 60, 62, 87, 90; frontier with China, 54–5; independence of, 56–7, 73; relations with China, 40, 54–61, 75, 87, 91, 100–1

Cambodia, 9, 25, 95; relations with China, 1, 25–9, 100–1

Cantonese, communities in Southeast Asia, 37

Capitalism, in Southeast Asia, 5, 83, 91

Champa, 7

Chiang Kai-shek, Chinese Nationalist leader, 10–11, 13, 34, 49, 69

Chou En-lai, Prime Minister of China, 14, 27, 40, 60, 81, 84, 85, 87, 89

Cultural Revolution, in China, 18, 21, 60, 71, 78, 86–8, 90–1, 93, 102

Diem, President Ngo Dinh, 15, 24

Dienbienphu, French defeat at, 13, 14

Djakarta, 40, 41, 96

Domino Theory, 95

Dutch, rule in Indonesia, 33, 34, 35, 37, 38

Education, of overseas Chinese. 88–9

France, recognition of People's Republic of China, 12; rule in Cambodia, 9, 25–6; rule in Laos, 9, 29, 31; rule in Vietnam, 9–15, 95; war with China (1883), 9

Fukien, 36.

Geneva, Conference at, 11, 14, 15, 16, 24, 26, 29, 35, 105

SELECT BIBLIOGRAPHY

Books

Aidit, D. N., *Indonesian Society and the Indonesian Revolution*, Djakarta, 1958.
Ambekar, G. V., (ed.) *Documents on China's relations with South and Southeast Asia* (1949–1962), Bombay, 1964.
Doak Barnett, A., *Communist China and Asia*, N.Y. 1960.
Clutterbuck, R. L., *The Long Long War: the emergency in Malaysia*, 1948–1960, London, 1967.
FitzGerald, C. P., *The Third China: the Chinese communities in Southeast Asia*, London, 1965.
FitzGerald, C. P., *The Chinese view of their place in the World*, London, 1966.
FitzGerald, C. P., *The Southern Expansion of the Chinese People*, Canberra, 1971.
FitzGerald, S. A., *China and the Overseas Chinese: A study of Peking's changing policy*, 1949–1970, Cambridge, 1972.
Girling, J. L. S., *People's War: the conditions and consequences in China and in Southeast Asia*, London, 1969.
Gurtov, Melvin, *China and Southeast Asia*, Lexington, 1971.
Halpern, A. M., (ed.) *Policies towards China: views from six continents*, N.Y. 1965.
Hinton, Harold C., *China's relations with Burma and Vietnam: a brief survey*, N.Y. 1958.
Hinton, Harold C., *Communist China in world politics*, Boston, 1966.
Hinton, Harold C., *China's Turbulent Quest: an analysis of China's Foreign relations since 1945*, N.Y. 1970.
Hsiung, James C., *Law and policy in China's foreign relations*, N.Y. 1971.
Johnston, D. M. and Chiu, Hungdah, *Agreements of the People's Republic of China 1949–1967: a calendar*, Cambridge, Mass. 1968.
Johnstone, William C., *Burma's Foreign Policy*, Cambridge, Mass. 1963.
Lee, Chae-jin, *Communist China's policy towards Laos: a case study, 1954–1967*, Lawrence, 1970.
O'Ballance, E., *Malaya: the Communist Insurgent War 1948–1960*, London, 1966.
Ojha, Ishwer C., *Chinese foreign policy in an age of transition: the diplomacy of cultural despair*, Boston, 1969.

Passin, Herbert, *China's Cultural diplomacy*, London, 1962.
Purcell, Victor, *The Chinese in Southeast Asia*, 2nd edn London, 1965.
Scalapino, Robert A., (ed.) *The Communist revolution in Asia*, Englewood Cliffs, N.J. 1969.
Simon, Sheldon W., *The Broken Triangle: Peking, Djakarta and the PKI*, Baltimore, Md. 1969.
Steiner, H. Arthur, *The International Position of Communist China*, N.Y. 1958.
Tsou, Tang, (ed.) *China in Crisis, vol. II, China's Policies in Asia and America's alternatives*, University of Chicago Press, 1968.
van Ness, P., *Revolution and Chinese Foreign Policy*, Berkeley, 1971.
Williams, L., *The Future of the Overseas Chinese in Southeast Asia*, N.Y. 1965.
Willmott, D. E., *The National Status of the Chinese in Indonesia, 1900–1958*, Cornell University Press, Ithaca, 1961.

Serials

Symposium on The Chinese in Southeast Asia, *The China Quarterly*, no. 20 (Oct.–Dec. 1964), 38–127.
'Communist China's Foreign Policy' Special issue of *Current History* vol. 33, no. 196 (Dec. 1957).
'Communist China in World Politics' Special issue of *Journal of International Affairs*, XI, no. 2 (1957).
Ministry of Foreign Affairs, *Chung-hua jen-min kung-ho kuo t'iao-yueh chi* (Collected Treaties of the People's Republic of China), Peking, 1957–
Shih-chieh chih-shih ch'u-pan she, *Chung-hua jen-min kung-ho Kuo tui-wai kuan-hsi wen-chien chi* (Documents on Foreign Affairs of the People's Republic of China) Peking, 1957–
Asian Survey (Berkeley, Cailfornia).
The China Quarterly (London).
Current Background (United States Consulate-General, Hong Kong).
Peking Review (Peking).
Shih-chieh chih-shih (Peking).